HOPE RISING

*To Melissa —
Wishing you
many Blessings*

Pam Witter

PAMELA H. WITTER

HOPE RISING

TATE PUBLISHING
AND ENTERPRISES, LLC

Hope Rising
Copyright © 2013 by Pamela H. Witter. All rights reserved.

No part of this publication may be reproduced, stored in a retrieval system or transmitted in any way by any means, electronic, mechanical, photocopy, recording or otherwise without the prior permission of the author except as provided by USA copyright law.

Scripture taken from the Contemporary English Version, Copyright © 1995 by American Bible Society. Used by permission.

This novel is a work of fiction. Names, descriptions, entities, and incidents included in the story are products of the author's imagination. Any resemblance to actual persons, events, and entities is entirely coincidental.

The opinions expressed by the author are not necessarily those of Tate Publishing, LLC.

Published by Tate Publishing & Enterprises, LLC
127 E. Trade Center Terrace | Mustang, Oklahoma 73064 USA
1.888.361.9473 | www.tatepublishing.com

Tate Publishing is committed to excellence in the publishing industry. The company reflects the philosophy established by the founders, based on Psalm 68:11,
"The Lord gave the word and great was the company of those who published it."

Book design copyright © 2013 by Tate Publishing, LLC. All rights reserved.
Cover design by Errol Villamante
Interior design by Honeylette Pino

Published in the United States of America

ISBN: 978-1-62746-896-1
1. Family & Relationships / General
2. Fiction / Family Life
13.07.31

DEDICATION

To Tom and Amelia with love.

PREFACE

An old friend recently shared a quote with me by literary editor and critic Norman Cousins. Cousins said, "Death is not the greatest loss in life. The greatest loss is what dies inside us while we live."

The quote troubled me. I wondered, why stop there? My response to her was, "The greatest thrill in life is resurrecting those things that have died inside us."

Hope Rising delves into the very real world of human brokenness. It explores raw, life-altering pain—the kind of pain that freezes time forever. Then it takes a bold step forward. *Hope Rising* challenges us to look beyond the moment when our soul is fractured; beyond the things that die inside us while we live. It fearlessly asserts that perseverance and faith can resurrect all that is good in us. Love. Peace. Wholeness. Joy. Hope. Innocence. Strength. It reminds us we have the capacity to transcend our pain. The only thing keeping us from healing is not knowing how.

In particular, *Hope Rising* explores the kind of sexual violence that impacts millions of men and women around the world today. While this is a work of fiction, I drew upon my own life experiences to paint an honest picture. This book truly is a work of my heart.

As you go on this journey with me and with Anastasia and Ellie—whether your life story includes our brand of brokenness or some other—I pray for your healing. I also ask for your prayers–prayers that others will find meaning in this story.

I wish you many blessings in the days ahead!

Kind regards,

Pamela H. Witter

Pamela H. Witter

INVADING THE DARKNESS

Anastasia heard the brakes on the school bus moan as it slowed in front of her house. She paused from packing and let out a deep sigh. There was no telling what kind of mood her daughter would be in. Since Ellie began the ninth grade two weeks ago, she had grown more sullen with each passing day.

The front door opened and Anastasia heard her daughter coming up the stairs. She dropped her white blouse into the suitcase on her bed and turned to say hello, but Ellie was already down the hallway. The bedroom door slammed shut, rattling the family photos on the wall.

The silence was killing Anastasia. She knew all about hiding secrets and the effect that had on a person's soul. Anastasia refused to see her daughter succumb to that kind of life. Day after day, she pushed for answers, but Ellie pushed back.

Anastasia walked down the hallway and slowly opened Ellie's bedroom door. Her daughter sat on an oversized bean bag chair, head in her hands, crying. Anastasia kneeled down and wrapped her arms around Ellie. "What is it honey," she pleaded.

Ellie leaned in. "It's Cassie," she said. Her best friend, Cassie, shunned her the first day of high school. Ellie was heart-broken. She and Cassie had been friends from the time they wore diapers, but they were drastically different girls. Cassie, *like,* loved to go to the mall and *totally* thought boys were *like* the hottest things ever! From kindergarten, Ellie would rather punch a boy in the arm. She played video games and aspired to be a rock singer…or maybe a food critic (but refused to eat anything containing vegetables). The demise of their friendship may have been inevitable, but how do you tell that to a fifteen-year-old?

As she shared the whole sordid tale with Anastasia, Ellie cried. Then her tears turned to anger. Ellie insisted she would not let anyone treat her that way. She planned on having words with Cassie. Anastasia admired Ellie's fearlessness. She herself had never been that way as a young teen. Quite the opposite, Anastasia was so timid as a girl, she often let people walk right through her. She did not want to discourage Ellie from having high standards, but she also did not want to get a phone call from the principal saying her daughter beat up her ex-best-friend.

"Listen, Ellie," Anastasia said, "I understand this hurts. Believe me, I do, but I do not want you getting into a fight with Cassie. If you cannot handle this in a positive way, I want you to give yourself some time to simmer down before you talk to her. Do you understand?"

Something snapped in Ellie. "Do you hate me, Mom?" she screamed. "I mean, really, do you want me to be a complete outcast? If I let Cassie do this now, when she's starting to hang out with the popular kids, I will never have a chance in high school. I can't do that, Mom. I won't!" She was already up off the floor and in seconds, bolted down the hallway. Anastasia watched in shock. She felt like a train had torn through the bedroom wall, stopping to rest directly in front of her face. Anastasia hated confrontation and Ellie never yelled at her before—not like that. Anastasia sighed. She understood exactly how Ellie was feeling, but getting her daughter to relate to her seemed an impossible feat. Ellie saw Anastasia as an outdated leftover from the eighties whose sole purpose was to provide lunch money and rides and whose idea of a good time was hanging out with "boring church people." What usable thing could Anastasia possibly have to offer? In Ellie's mind, they operated in different galaxies. No comparison existed.

She tried to talk to her daughter one last time before the two-hour drive to Buffalo, where Anastasia would board an airplane for a work trip to Baltimore. Ellie, however, refused to come down from the treefort in the backyard. Her dad built it for her when she was nine and it came in handy during moments like these. Anastasia called Aaron on his cell phone before she pulled out of the driveway and let him know what was going on. He would be home in the next hour or so. He would have no problem getting Ellie back into the house and calmed down. He had a special way with her. Anastasia, however, felt troubled the entire trip. Unsettled problems left her mind messy.

Two days later, Anastasia sat on the puffy white comforter that covered the queen-size bed in her hotel room. She stared out of the enormous picture window at the Baltimore cityscape. Lights shined in the windows of adjacent buildings. Cars darted by below. Little dots moved about like ants, going into shops and restaurants and chatting with friends. All of the activity outside contrasted the solitude in her room. The only remnant that made it to her ears from the maelstrom below was a hum that bounced off the outside of the thick-paneled glass and evaporated into the blue-and-white sky.

Inside the room she sensed a buzz, like a high-pitched sound only dogs could hear. She wondered if anyone else noticed it. The buzzing, she determined, resulted from room after room after room being wired and remote controlled. She imagined she was in a metal-by-wooden womb where hundreds of people ate, slept, walked, swam, watched television, and talked furiously into cell phones, land lines, and computer video feeds.

The street lights below blinked far beyond her reach, and the buildings and houses looked like cardboard boxes containing thousands of souls—living, breathing, alive. Despite it, Anastasia's little box on the twenty-third floor sat quietly dormant. She felt markedly alone.

During a different time in her life, that loneliness might have sent Anastasia into a panic, as if the four white walls were closing in on her. Then she would disappear into the darkness; but so much had changed since her youth—changes she could not have anticipated. She had learned not to run from her loneliness—from any feeling for that matter. Anastasia focused on her breathing. With each exhale she became self-aware, leaving behind the busy world beneath her. She focused on the sound of air leaving her lungs until she completely returned to the present moment. Anastasia prayed the prayer she spoke every single day of her life for the last decade.

"Lord, thank you," she whispered out loud. "I give everything to you. All that I have is yours. Please use me for your purposes. Protect me. Protect my family and keep us safe. Amen."

The Spirit stirred within her. It always remained, no matter where her work took her. In the midst of chaos or in silent loneliness, it surrounded her and lived within her. She held tight to the sound of her breath and reveled in the peace she felt at that moment. While her earthly family moved about hundreds of miles away, the Spirit connected them over the distance and kept her company. She could not wait for morning; for a short bus ride to the airport, a slightly frightening take-off over the east-coast landscape, and an hour and a half drive back to the deep countryside of Western New York. She could not wait for hugs and kisses, a messy house, a drooling dog, and the peace of the foothills; but until then, she felt comforted by her prayers. As the sun set and the water around the city reflected a blazing pink sky, Anastasia drifted off to sleep.

In her dreams she saw a twenty-year-old version of herself rocking back and forth, arms wrapped around her legs. She sat in a small living room in a cold, dark apartment. Paint peeled in patches from the walls. A tiny spot of blackish-green mold escaped out beneath the corner of the linoleum in the kitchen. One lamp cast shadows from a rickety wooden side-table next to the only decent piece of furniture in the place—a brown and caramel-colored love seat her Grandma left her. In Anastasia's dream, tears dripped like rain down her cheeks.

A sound overtook her space – the sound of breathing. It was rapid, shallow.

She moaned, shaking her head back and forth. Suddenly, this younger Anastasia burst into motion. She ran for the white front door, shoved it open and leaped out. She ran down Maple Street to Union and all the way to the river along Chamberlain Park. She ran under the trestle and threw herself down on the giant rocks lining the riverbank. She was alone in the shadows. Anastasia leaned forward and let the cold water run across her fingertips. She closed her eyes and inhaled crisp air. As the crystal clear water passed over the gold colored rocks below, Anastasia smiled. She imagined dropping down into the current and swimming away like a fish.

No one came. In the dream, she sat and sat for a long time. She sat until the bells at St. John's Church chimed six o'clock. Louder and louder and louder, the church bells rang until they were all she could hear.

Anastasia awoke from her dream, her cheeks damp. The alarm clock was buzzing. It had felt so real. Anastasia remembered the feeling from her dream. It suddenly struck her—there was a time she wanted to leave the world behind simply to escape her pain. Now, she looked forward to leaving the world, but not until it *was* her time. She looked forward to becoming whole; returning to the one who made her. Anastasia also realized she had taken giant leaps from those younger years, when the darkness inside her hurt so badly it caused her to run.

As she sat upright in the big hotel bed, Anastasia thought of Ellie back home. A photo of Ellie and Aaron sat on the nightstand. Anastasia always carried it during her travels; placing it on the nightstand to make her feel more at home. In the photo, Ellie and Aaron stood by the driver's side door of Aaron's truck. The sun reflected on the sparkly blue-grey paint. Aaron wore a big smile in the shadow of his tattered baseball cap.

Ellie leaned sideways, one leg in the air. Her dad held her up as she stretched out her arms in a big V-shape. She was laughing, her brown hair tossed back and her eyes nearly squeezed shut. Anastasia loved that picture. Ellie and Aaron were her two favorite people in the entire world. She could look at that picture ten thousand times and smile with each new glance.

Anastasia leaned over and hit snooze on the alarm clock. She pushed herself back down into the massive comforter and nestled her head into the perfectly fluffy pillow. Sleep came quickly. The second round of buzzing came even quicker.

Anastasia worked for a small Christian college and had made a number of donor visits in Baltimore, but the trip was two-fold. She also addressed a group of about 200 women on the interaction between humanity and the divine on the earthly plane and how faithful discipleship grows those interactions in our daily lives. She was well received and spent some time autographing her devotional book and chatting with the ladies afterwards. It felt like weeks since she arrived, yet it had been little more than forty-eight hours.

Now she went through her normal post-visit routine. Copy all of her notes into her laptop. Write thank-you letters to drop in the mailbox back in New York. Take a shower. Blow-dry and style her hair. Put on makeup. Thoroughly sweep the room for any stray items. Make the bed. Pack. Carry everything down to the hotel lobby. Check out. Eat breakfast. Depart.

On the plane, the roar of the twin engines rocked them forward with a jerk at first; then, as the giant metal craft gained speed down the runway, the pressure pushed her back in her seat. It lifted with a touch of turbulent motion before gaining ground by the miles until it was gliding over a carpet of clouds below. Take off terrified her. Landing terrified her. However, the flight itself soothed her as she glanced out of the window at what looked like an entire landscape made out of pulled-apart cotton balls, covered on top with a strikingly-soft blue sky. As the plane settled into perpetual motion, she leaned back in the seat and stretched her legs out in front of her. Anastasia's mind wandered back to Ellie. An idea came to her. "Write Ellie a letter. Tell her my story." Anastasia stood up and reached into the front pocket of her carry-on bag. She pulled out a small white pad of paper and a pen. The words came quickly.

BROKEN SILENCE

Dear Ellie,

There are a lot of things I never told you; things you might want to know now. I hope it will help you understand me better, help us to get back to being close. It's too hard to talk about, so I'm writing it down for you. It's my story, baby—our family's story. In a way, it's your story too. Here goes.

My grey-blue eyes nearly matched the color of the sky that day, or at least it felt that way. I stared out of the third-floor window in my eighth-grade math class. I used to love that class; I had actually been pushed forward a year for doing so well in sixth grade; but that day, the noise hurt my head. The side of a steep hill stared back at me from outside the window. Brown earth bulged out from beneath green clumps. Just a handful of weeks before, that hillside looked like a soft carpet of grass. I had laid on it after school one day, drawn to its plush façade and its beautiful solitude. Pounding rain and devastating winds had since destroyed its surface, signifying the arrival of fall.

I understood that devastation on a deep, personal level. In fact, I had a good reason for counting the days until the end of fall. The season had swept away more than cushiony grass on a hillside. It swept away my soul, my desire to feel, my self-worth, my happiness, and most of all, my innocence. Like most kids, they were things I was not even aware I possessed until I lost them. Fall represented the devastation of nature and simultaneously, the strategic deconstruction of my life without any warning at all. At least winter was blatantly and consistently cold. That I could handle.

It began on the first day of school. A boy I previously never noticed caught my eye and held it for a second too long. His were a transparent blue and he had long red hair—like a juvenile rock star. My crush began small but cascaded into a raging river. I fell asleep at night picturing him in the hallway, wearing a black t-shirt and jeans, brushing his hair out of his eyes with a smile that said, "I know you better than you know yourself." Turns out, he did.

On a Friday afternoon, my friend Carlynn—a more experienced young girl who had convinced me to smoke my first cigarette—pulled me into the bathroom between classes. I never completely liked being around Carlynn. It made me feel dirty, but somehow Carlynn always found "that thing" that lured me in.

"Guess what," she exclaimed.

I knew Carlynn's excitement would reveal something good, mixed with a touch of bad. Skeptically, I answered, "What is it?"

"Ricky and Reece are coming over to my house tonight."

Her words sat on top of the air between us, staring me directly in the face. Carlynn awaited a reaction, a response of some kind, but I just stared at her.

"Well, are you going to sleep over tonight or what?" Carlynn asked.

"Umm…why?"

"Oh my God, duh! Reece is coming over to see you. My mom has to work late. Ricky thought it would be fun if the four of us hung out."

"But doesn't Reece have a girlfriend," I asked with exaggerated inflections. "Last I knew he was dating Jenna. My God, she's the prettiest girl in my English class. Why in the world would he want to hang out with me?"

"I know," Carlynn answered, smiling nervously like a kid caught with her hand in the cookie jar before supper. "Who knows. They must have broken up. Just sleep over. We'll hang out and talk and you can get to know him better. You can ask about Jenna yourself."

My mind raced. Carlynn and Ricky were pretty involved. Reece and Ricky were good friends. Would he expect the same thing out of me? Plus, they would probably be drinking, and essentially I would be lying to my parents by withholding the fact that Carlynn's mom was working late. It felt wrong. I was about to listen to that inner voice and say no when the bell rang for class.

Mrs. Greenridge walked through the door. "Get to your rooms girls," she demanded. We ran out of the bathroom toward gym.

By the end of the day, I passed by Reece twice in the hallway. Both times, he stared at me far too long. The second time, he walked slowly passed and whispered, "See you tonight?" His voice felt like warm melted caramel over vanilla ice cream.

"Yeah," I breathed, without even realizing I had changed my mind.

My mom dropped me off at Carlynn's house at exactly five o'clock. Mrs. Dealton was already gone to work. She would be gone most of the night. The restaurant where she waitressed was packed on Friday nights. They served the best fried fish in town.

Carlynn and I spent the early part of the evening looking through yearbooks, giggling at the pictures of ourselves with "big" hair. "We were such dorks," I laughed. We called a couple of friends and talked about our favorite television stars. We pulled out her mom's curling iron and played around with new hairstyles.

"This is fun," I thought. I felt great, but all that giggly, girly happiness halted when the doorbell rang. I had almost forgotten why I came. My heart flooded with guilt. "My parents won't like this," I thought. Then another part of me countered, "But we're just hanging out. It's not a big deal." Adrenaline rushed through my body when the boys walked in. They were different than most boys our age. They had rough older brothers in high school. They didn't participate in any school functions. They were always in the background, watching. In the mornings, I saw them at the baseball dugouts smoking cigarettes. Carlynn said they smoked weed there sometimes too. Reece's oldest brother, who was in his early twenties, had gone to jail for selling pills to some high school kids.

I also noticed during those first weeks of school that they seemed a lot older than fourteen. It was their eyes—they always looked like they were searching for something, and they were. Their eyes sought weakness.

As soon as he walked in, Reece immediately stared long and hard at me. I fluttered a bit, brushing my long blonde hair back nervously and looking down at my stark white sneakers. "What is happening," I thought. "Two days ago I had never been this close to him and he was walking down the hall with his girlfriend. He was my fantasy. Now it feels like we're the only people here."

The rest of the evening played out like a silent Chaplin movie. This is where the story gets tough, Ellie. I hope you can make it through to the end.

Within minutes, Carlynn and Ricky disappeared into the back bedroom. It made me uncomfortable, but Reece just laughed. We sat on the couch, far apart from one another. Reece made small talk before pulling a six-pack out of his book bag. I wondered where he got it but didn't ask. If I asked, I would sound like I couldn't get beer myself. I felt compelled to act casual. That was a huge mistake.

Reece pulled a can away from the whitish-clear plastic rings. It jerked out with a snap. He shoved the cold can into my hand and cracked open the top. Drops of beer sprayed my forearm.

"Thanks," I murmured and took a long drink. It was disgusting, but I drank it anyway. One full can in and my mind was already buzzing and my vision blurred. Another half a can and I couldn't bear to taste anymore of it. Reece grabbed my hand and pulled me up off the couch. "C'mon," he demanded, "let's check the place out."

We wandered around the first floor until we found a stairway off of the kitchen leading down into the basement. I remembered following Carlynn down there once to throw the laundry on the floor beside the washer. It wasn't a terrible basement. It was cold, with a white cement floor and rough-painted stone walls. Reece yanked my hand as he danced down the stairs, flicking on a light switch along the way.

"There's nothing exciting down here," I said nervously, but he didn't seem to hear me. I felt like I was watching myself in a movie, featuring plain old me and this teenage heartthrob. It was unreal. Reece looked around for a second or two before grabbing my arm and spinning me around to face him.

Startled, I laughed nervously. Reece wasted no time. He wrapped his arms around me, and without a moment's hesitation he dropped me to the small piece of remnant carpet on the floor. He pushed his hands aggressively to places they should not have been. I pushed back trying to stop him, but he threw off my resistance as if I were a toddler. It was no surprise. I weighed about a hundred pounds to his one-sixty. I found out later that Reece had been held back two years in grade school. He was sixteen to my fourteen, and a big sixteen at that.

My mind screamed, "No," but my mouth was paralyzed. Words did not exist except in my head. In that moment, all of my passive, timid ways merged into a solitary being inside my body, holding me back. "This is not happening. This is not happening," it kept saying, over and over and over again. Then silence filled the room as Reece pushed himself on top of me. His rapid breathing filled my ears. Pain seared through my body.

I turned and looked at the wall. A bright orange picture of a flower hung above the washing machine. I kept my eyes on that picture and went numb. The rest of the evening never happened. Life stopped at that very moment as I succumbed to the silence inside myself.

Reece left with Ricky that night, but I did not see him go. Carlynn slapped me proudly on the back and congratulated me for "taking the leap." "It's about damn time," Carlynn laughed, not noticing the emptiness staring back at her.

The next morning, I called my mother at the crack of dawn to come and pick me up. "What's wrong, honey?" Mom asked. "Is everything okay? Why are you calling so early?"

"Mom, I don't feel good. Carlynn is so stupid, and I just want to be home. Please come get me."

Mom arrived in the driveway before 7:00 a.m., and I was back in my own bed by 7:30. I stayed there the rest of the weekend, claiming a mild flu. Monday morning came quicker than I wanted it to. My mom insisted I was well enough for school. That blue-and-white sweater I always wore looked so childish now, and too tight. It constricted me in ways some girls enjoyed, but not me. I wished I were a boy with a flat chest, devoid of curves. I despised my body.

I rummaged through my drawers until I found a big, old t-shirt I had gotten at the amusement park last year and pulled it on with a pair of ripped jeans—ones I had previously not worn out of the backyard. I pasted my toothbrush and looked into the mirror, catching a glimpse of my eyes.

I barely recognized myself. In fact, the old Anastasia was completely gone. No one would notice, but I did. This new one troubled me. I felt a sort of hatred for her. A tear tickled my lips. "Dumb girl," I sneered. "Silly, stupid girl."

At school, the wide hallway lined with lockers felt like a beehive buzzing with ultra-hyper, happy students. They darted in every direction. "Please don't let him see me," my mind whispered. "Maybe he'll avoid his locker between classes; avoid me." I deliberately walked more quickly than usual. Two feet from my escape route a shoulder connected hard with mine sending my books tumbling to the floor. I dropped to one knee, glancing up and back to see who had been so rude.

Long red hair. "No," my mind pleaded. Black t-shirt. "No." Blue jeans. "No!" Smirking, he turned and looked right at me, one hand tucked into Jenna's back pocket. "No," I screamed in my head as they wisped by, crushing my brain into a muddy pulp. My eyes moved from Reece to his girlfriend. Jenna's innocence was perfectly intact. It bubbled over as her long, golden curls bounced around her shoulders. Only three days ago, I had been just as unaware as Jenna of the darkness in people's hearts, but not anymore. In fact, that darkness behaved like a virus transmitted from its carrier to anyone whom they exposed. I had been so vulnerable.

In that hallway between classes, Reece stared into my eyes—perhaps for eternity—and slowly killed me with his smile. He winked as he turned the corner. I turned a corner too—one I never saw coming. In that moment, darkness flooded every fiber of my being. It surged into my heart like tar. It filled my head, leaving me dumb and lifeless. It emptied my body of all light, except the bright white spots of an impending migraine. I would battle those headaches for twelve years. I blinked away the pain before heat waves blurred my vision, and I collapsed against the wall. I never told a soul about Reece.

Ellie, don't make my mistakes. Don't bury your feelings deep down inside, and don't let other people's inflictions cause you to become dark. Don't play the game. I know your friend hurt you, honey. I know this is new. How do we move beyond our pain when we first realize that people can be ugly; that someone we love and trust can cause us harm? I do understand what it feels like to be betrayed. I know what it feels like to be an outcast. You can trust me, sweetie. You can talk to me.

Love,
Mom

Anastasia debated with herself all the rest of the way home – from the plane to her car to her driveway on Stony Creed Road. "Is it too much," she asked herself. "I don't know if a teenager can handle this." Anastasia decided not to give the letter to Ellie. Maybe she would try talking about it first, and if Ellie seemed mature enough to handle it, she would share it all, or maybe she would hold onto this and give it to Ellie later when she was an adult, or never at all. She pushed the pad of paper down into her purse.

Inside, Aaron sat sprawled on his camouflage recliner. Ellie plugged away at the newest version of her favorite role-playing video game. The dog bounded excitedly toward Anastasia, his nails clicking on the wooden floor in the kitchen, and practically leaped into her arms. She played with him for a moment then walked in to the living room. Despite what had happened before she left, Aaron and Ellie jumped out of their seats and tackled her with hugs. She smiled and hugged them back fiercely. She was home, and all was well.

A SECOND STORM

Back at the office, Anastasia played catch-up. Twenty-five emails. A to-do list thirty items long. Several voicemail messages. People in and out. Working at a Christian college thrilled Anastasia. It allowed her to have a solid career supporting a mission she could really sink her teeth into. She loved the idea of seeing young people make the transition from youth to adulthood in a healthy and safe environment where their beliefs could become their own, where they not only pursued their profession but contemplated deep, life-changing questions along the way. Her career at the school also enhanced her writing and speaking abilities. It allowed her a nice salary and benefits package while instilling a desire for lifelong learning that pushed her to new aspirations. Anastasia had learned to blog there. Her position often required her to speak publicly. She had interacted with what she thought to be some of the greatest theological minds of her time. The college community and her peers in particular challenged her to new levels of personal growth that felt to Anastasia like the final exclamation point on years of intense transition.

She worked furiously, as if Monday were the last at-bat in a tie game with bases loaded. Around 4:00, as she entered the final stretch, her stomach growled. "Dinner in two hours," she told herself. "No snacks." By the time the clock on her computer read 5:00, her list was cut in half. With a big sigh, she stretched her neck and sat back in her chair, watching the computer shut down.

Her thoughts wandered to her story, the one she started for Ellie. It felt so good to get it down on paper—like therapy. She still did not intend to give the letter to her daughter, especially after things went so well the night before; however, the process of writing it intrigued her. She did not have to pick up Ellie from her guitar lesson until 6:00. She had about a half hour to kill. Anastasia pulled the pad out of her purse, grabbed a blue ink pen from her desk drawer, shook it, and began to write.

Dear Ellie,

I don't know why I'm doing this. I have known you since you took your first breath. I like to think I know you inside and out. I watched you giggle at the silliest things when you were a baby, eating creamed food in your high chair. I watched you struggle through second grade. I watched you fall in love for the first time at the age of eight and helped you through it when your feelings got hurt. I saw you grow into a beautiful young lady, and I imagine all your future holds. Maybe I want you to know me that well—know who I was and how I came to be who I am today. Maybe I want you to feel like you can relate to me. Maybe I'm not writing this for you at all, but for myself. I don't know. Nevertheless, I feel like writing.

High school sucked. After Reece, the darkness inside me seemed to radiate outward and alienate me from everything normal. The looks, the comments, the teasing all left me empty. I often walked to school alone along the train tracks, a pair of headphones strapped to my ears, cranking the latest Rage Against the Machine song. The anger in the lyrics gave me something I could not come to on my own. I never lashed out after Reece. I sunk in. The music spoke all of my anger for me.

As I left the tracks behind, crossed Hill Street, and entered the lengthy field that led to the high school, something struck my back. It stung, and I spun around to see what happened. Two older boys jogged toward me, rocks in hand. I took off like a cat when snarling dogs step out slowly from a darkened garage.

The chase was on. They ran faster than I did and gained ground more quickly than I expected. I had hoped to make it to the fence behind the middle school where there was a small opening I could fit through. They would be stuck on the other side. However, they reached me as I rounded the corner to the back of the building. Bad idea. No adult could see us there.

I spun around and walked in reverse until my back hit the brick wall. "Come on, you guys, leave me alone," I pleaded. They laughed. No hope for me. The rocks dropped from their hands, thudding as they hit the ground.

Craig was a junior and a football player. He squinted his eyes and lowered his head. "Dude, what the hell is wrong with you," he asked.

I said nothing.

"Yo, Joe, I bet no one has ever touched this chick. Who would, right? She's so freaking weird."

Joe laughed. "Yeah, but look, man, she has a nice little body, right?"

My heart pounded so hard it made me sick to my stomach. Old feelings swirled through my bloodstream. Old memories. Fear of a repeat performance. I wretched.

The boys' eyes widened as I vomited brutally in front of them. "Sick," Joe yelled. "That's nasty."

"Go smoke another one," Craig shouted and picked the rock back up. He thrust it at me, striking me in the shoulder, immediately leaving a painful red welt. They ran off, cat-calling as their voices faded in the distance. To them it was a moment of entertainment in an otherwise boring day. To me, it fractured my soul.

School remained like this for some time. I found solace in drugs and alcohol. They kept my secret from being real—as if darkness were a choice rather than a sickness inflicted upon me because of my own weakness. I drowned myself in a world of chosen self-destruction so no one would see just how truly worthless I felt.

I began cutting. The first time it was with a friend. She told me in secret that she started the year before. It felt so good to her; I could see it in her eyes. She handed me the sharp, black-handled knife with a smile. It was like she knew I needed it. I pushed the silver blade into my white forearm skin and blood pooled up around the tip. I pulled.

The pain was sharp and hot. It stung. I pulled more. Red streaks circled around my forearm in lines. I pulled, and as I did, a steam release valve opened up inside my head. I cried—not because it hurt. It felt so amazing.

As life spilled down the hallways of junior high, high school, and into the streets of adulthood, I died a thousand deaths—feeling alive temporarily by the pain I inflicted on myself. I became what Reece's eyes saw—good for one thing and one thing only. His deception would certainly not be the last lie I believed.

Ellie, you know that I think good and evil are very real. I believe in God and Satan, in angels and demons. I did not back then. I just thought life was like a giant tidal wave and I was sitting on my rickety wooden raft holding on, trying not to disappear as the water crested the horizon. I had no idea then that the evil in our world fathered all lies. The deception I was under could be broken. I had no idea I could simply step off the raft, walk across the water, and find my way to a peaceful island and a bed of warm sand. It took a long time to discover that simple truth. I suffered a lot because of that deception.

I think I was about fifteen the next time lightning struck. My good friend Samantha invited me to sleep over. Her mom was different. She had short, feathered blonde hair and square shoulders. She walked with heavy steps and talked in short sentences. She never made dinner for us or asked if we needed anything. Usually she stayed away. This particular night, Samantha's adult brother Gerry hung around the house. He came in from out of state to visit for a couple weeks. Samantha speculated his wife kicked him out and he was giving her time to simmer down. Gerry called Samantha's uncle to come over and watch the game with him. The three of us girls played Monopoly at the dining room table while Gerry and Uncle Alex shouted at the television set.

After I had taken all of the girls' money, Samantha wandered into the living room and shouted, "Turn it down, for Pete's sake. The TV is too loud."

Her uncle Alex looked up at us and grinned. He was extremely drunk by then. "Are you pregnant?" he asked me.

"What," I responded, incredulous, before looking down at my stomach. I was a tiny girl, but had terrible posture, mostly because I never wanted my chest to stick out. My stomach did look like a little pouch. I straightened right up and his eyes immediately moved to my chest. I ran upstairs, nearly crying.

"You're an asshole," Samantha shouted.

Upstairs we forgot about the guys for a while. We drew pictures of our favorite band logos on our school notebooks and lightning bolts and peace signs on our jeans. We heard a car door slam shut in the driveway below. "Must be Uncle Al leaving, thank God," Samantha said. With the coast clear, we went downstairs for a snack.

The guys stood whispering in the living room. "I thought you left," Samantha said to Alex. "No, your mom did," he answered. "She's going out to meet her girlfriend," he taunted.

"It's not her girlfriend," Samantha shrieked.

This was not good. When Samantha's mom went out, she usually did not come back. I would often stay until noon the following day, with no Mrs. Trenton in sight. Who knows where she went or what she did, but she certainly did not worry about us girls. Sometimes we left the house and wandered the streets. Other times we stayed in and called boys on the phone. This night, my heart feared the worst.

The evening passed slowly as we holed up in Samantha's room, avoiding the ruckus downstairs. About midnight, we put on our pajamas and climbed into bed. Samantha and I shared her bed, which was a queen-size mattress on the floor. Our friend Tammy decided to sleep in the spare bedroom just down the hall.

Sometime in the night, we heard the door slam shut to the spare room. It was not a complete surprise. Tammy really liked older guys, and she was extremely sexually active. She had been flirting with Samantha's brother throughout the evening and joked that she was going to hook up with him. We heard muffled noises and giggled.

Samantha's room was so dark. The lack of light made my head spin a little when I opened my eyes, so I closed them tight and let myself drift off. As I slept, I felt Samantha moving away from me toward the edge of the bed. Then there was a bigger shake in the mattress. I opened my eyes and moved closer to Samantha, to make out her face.

It wasn't Samantha. Uncle Alex had squeezed in between us, and Samantha didn't seem to notice at all. She snored gently. To this day I wonder if she let it happen, if she gave me to him so that he would not bother her. Perhaps he had done this before.

"There's nowhere else to sleep," he whispered. "Your friend is in there with Gerry, and I was supposed to sleep in the spare room tonight. I'm just going to crash with you guys." He was so creepy.

"Just go sleep on the couch," I whispered, panicked.

"It hurts my back," he replied.

I closed my eyes so tight it made my head ache and pretended it was just me and Samantha in the room. Uncle Alex wasted little time. He grabbed my hand and whispered, "Be quiet, understand?"

I froze. Time froze. Uncle Alex put my hand on his stomach and moved it slowly passed the belt of his jeans. He didn't rape me. Instead, he made me touch him. I still wonder if it was because he feared I might be pregnant. I cried the entire time. All traces of humanity trickled away.

 Ten years later I drove by a little house on North Seventeenth Street and saw Uncle Alex playing with his two kids in the yard. His wife looked on lovingly from the front porch. My heart screamed out in pain. I wanted to crank the wheel sideways and veer off the road, crashing into his body. I imagined pinning it against a tree, but his kids were beautiful and innocent. I couldn't hurt them. I thought of jumping out of the car and running right up the front steps, grabbing his wife by the arm, and yelling, "Do you know what he did? Do you know?" Instead, I drove slowly by, watching him toss a round ball into the air and laugh. I hated him.

Anastasia looked up at her watch, startled. Fifteen minutes to get to Olean and pick up Ellie. Not enough time. She threw the pad of paper back in her purse and hurried out the door.

RIVERS RISING

In town, Ellie stood outside of the Rick's Rockin' Guitar Den. A young man of about twenty-five stood beside her, back straight, hands tucked in his pockets. He looked vaguely familiar, but he wasn't Rick. Ellie shuffled her feet across the dirt on the sidewalk.

"Ellie," Anastasia called from the driver's side window, "C'mon honey. We have to get home for supper."

"Mom," she hollered back. "Mr. Seeley wants to talk to you first."

"Ahhh, Mr. Seeley," Anastasia thought. "He's a teacher at the school."

Anastasia climbed out of the car door, up the curb, and made her way to her daughter and the English teacher. "Ellie, go sit in the car and wait for me," Anastasia said softly.

"Mr. Seeley, why are you at Ellie's guitar lesson? Shouldn't you be home?"

Mr. Seeley looked at Anastasia for a moment, contemplating his words carefully.

"Ma'am," he began.

"Call me Anastasia, please," she interrupted.

"Anastasia, something happened at school today. I didn't turn Ellie in. I dealt with it on my own. That's why I'm here. I told her I wanted to talk to you about it—that was my condition for not sending her to the principal's office." he said.

"What happened, Mr. Seeley?" she asked.

"Call me Terry," he said. "I walked out the side door of the school this afternoon and found Ellie smoking. She didn't see me at first. I watched for a minute and saw Ellie writing a poem. I came up behind her and startled her, I guess. I was just going to tell her to put the cigarette out. You know—no smoking on school property and all. She dropped the paper and I picked it up. The poem was really dark. It was about her friend. Ellie told me what happened. I'm afraid if this feud goes on much longer, Ellie might end up in a fight. She's a tough girl, Anastasia. She wouldn't hesitate to put someone in their place if they pushed too hard. In some ways, that's a good thing. School is tough. It's no cakewalk, but I don't want to see Ellie's education jeopardized because of this. I was hoping you could talk some sense into her."

Anastasia stared at Terry. "Smoking…she started smoking?" Things were worse than she thought. Ellie was writing "dark" poetry and smoking. Anastasia knew full well that what is on the surface of a person is but a smoke-cloud compared to what is inside.

"I'll talk to Ellie tonight," she said. "Thank you. Thank you for not turning her in and for coming to me." she asked, "Will you let me know how she's doing in school?"

"You bet," he answered."I appreciate it, Terry," Anastasia said. "Ellie's having a really tough time figuring out where she fits in this world. I'm not exactly sure how to help her; but I have some ideas."

The two departed and Anastasia returned to the car. She and Ellie drove in silence the entire way home. In the driveway, Ellie's hand moved quickly to the door handle. Anastasia reached out and stopped her.

"Ellie, I want to talk to you about something."

"Mom, I don't need a lecture about smoking. I've only had a couple. I won't do it again, God."

Anastasia reached in her purse and pulled out the pad that she had written on. Her heart raced. She handed it to Ellie, got out of the car, and walked inside to cook dinner. Ellie didn't come inside. An hour passed. Her dinner sat on a plate in the microwave. When Anastasia peeked out the window, Ellie was no longer in the car. She had moved to the tree fort.

Anastasia wandered out through the back yard and made her way up the wooden ladder. There was more than enough room for two. "Mom," she said before Anastasia had fully emerged from the hole in the floor, "Why did you tell me all that stuff?"

"I'm not sure honey," Anastasia answered. "I feel like you are going through some really difficult things right now. I'm not sure how to help you, baby. I love you so much; my chest aches when I think of you being unhappy. I wanted you to know that…. that I have been there. I might be able to help."

Ellie began to cry. Anastasia moved quietly beside her and held out her arms. Ellie nestled her head onto Anastasia's shoulder and sat that way for ten minutes. Ellie's cries slowed, and eventually her sobs returned to soft and gentle breathing.

"What's wrong Ellie?" Anastasia whispered.

"Mom, I don't know what to do. I'm on the brink. I am completely friendless right now. Cassie abandoned me and is hanging out with all these people we mutually disliked. Here I am on my own, and the only people who are nice to me are people who I know do bad things. Why is that? Am I weirdo, Mom?"

Anastasia stared at her beautiful little girl. She might be a teenager in high school, but she was still Anastasia's little sweetheart.

"Let's talk about Cassie first. Why is she doing this? Why is she working so hard to be friends with important people? Why is she giving up someone she loves for status? Ellie, people are going to make those kinds of choices throughout your entire life. I think Cassie is trying to fill some need in herself—some empty place. It doesn't give her the right to hurt you, but she will nevertheless. I feel sad for Cassie. Ellie, you are a strong young woman. It's hard for you to understand because you would never compromise yourself for status or for power or for money. So it hurts, right? And when it hurts, you want to make the hurt stop. Anger makes the hurt stop."

"Yeah, that makes sense, but what do you know about anger. I mean, your story—you never stood up for yourself. Maybe if you had, none of that would have happened to you. Maybe if you had kicked that Reece right square in his balls he would have left you alone. How do you know fighting isn't the answer?"

Anastasia's eyes widened. She was not accustomed to hearing her daughter speak that way. "Oh Ellie, that's just the beginning of the story. Can you give me some time ; let me gather my thoughts, and I'll tell you the rest. In the meantime though, you need to make me a promise. Can you do that?" Ellie nodded.

"No cigarettes. No fights. Promise you'll press pause until we get through all of this. Then—and I mean this—you can decide for yourself what the best response is. Can you promise me that?"

Ellie nodded again.

"And Ellie," Anastasia continued, "you are *not* a weirdo. You are intense. You are intelligent and busy. The games you play keep your mind sharp and focused. That's why you like them. You need immense stimulation because you are gifted, honey. Don't let anyone make you feel bad about that. You know

I have been saying this for ages, but God granted you an artistic side, something I never had. Keep using that. Find ways to be creative with all of these feelings. Don't succumb to the lies, to the images other people try to impose on you. Be stronger than them. Mental strength will get you so much farther in life."

Mother and daughter walked back to the house together. Ellie ate her supper. They snuggled on the couch and enjoyed an unusually light and airy evening together with Aaron, watching funny movies and laughing at the best parts. Anastasia could not wipe the smile off her face as she and Aaron lay in bed that night. Despite all of her fears, the story was working.

BIRTH OF LIES

Anastasia rolled into the parking space at the far end of the lot outside of the First Baptist Church. It was a small-town church, but a busy one. Around a hundred and fifty people attended each week, filling the modest-sized sanctuary with the tall stained glass windows.

It was a friendly church. Everyone hugged and shook hands and patted one another's backs. Like anywhere, naysayers came and went, but the negative energy never lasted long. It had no power over the love and happiness that permeated the hearts of most of the attendees. The mainstays of the church held fast and tight to keeping it a hub of fellowship and mutual support. Those who weren't on board usually left on their own before long.

This Wednesday evening, Anastasia led a small writer's circle. A mixed group gathered on couches and lounge chairs in a large half circle. After a brief devotional, the group took turns sharing their recent writings with one another. Mrs. Castle penned a prayer, a lovely one full of imagery and thankfulness. As she read it, her voice trembled with age, but her inflections emphasized the wisdom of the piece in all the right places. A perfect start to the evening.

The youngest member of the group, an eighteen-year-old college student, wrote a poem. It captured the inevitable growing pains of youth in a way that pulled tears from Anastasia's eyes. Yet it reflected a hopefulness that seemed to come from deep, honest faith. This girl was worlds ahead of Anastasia at that age, and it made Anastasia gleam with pride for her.

When it came to Anastasia, she pulled a yellow legal pad from her church bag. "I've been thinking about a new topic," she said. "I want to bounce the beginning off you guys and get your feedback. It is part of a talk I'm giving this winter. It's called Return to Innocence." Anastasia began.

A man and a woman stood naked in the midst of a lush utopia. Two trees, tall and grand, marked the center of the garden. On every branch, beautiful, radiant fruit hung. The breeze caught their sweet smell, carried it across the treetops, and rained it down on the earth below. One gave wisdom. The other afforded eternal life. God walked in the garden. He loved Adam and Eve, and they loved him. Out of love, God asked them not to eat the fruit on the grand old trees. He knew if they did they would be forever changed. They would not be able to stay in the garden. Outside the garden, Adam and Eve would become mortal beings, living in deterioration toward eventual death, but inside the garden—in God's holy presence—Adam and Eve possessed perfect health, perfect innocence, and perfect love.

But God had an enemy. Just as God's spirit took shape to walk and talk in the garden with Adam and Eve, His enemy did the same—a snake that sought to defy God and to defile God's perfect creation. One day, when God was away, the snake slithered up to naked, innocent Eve. She kneeled gently to the ground, her ear to the slick snake's mouth. It spoke. The snake hissed humanity's first lie.

"Eat that apple. You won't die," he said. "You will know more things, like God."

That sparkling, shiny, sweet-smelling fruit stared down at Eve. "Wisdom doesn't sound so bad," she must have thought. "Why not be more like God?" So naive, so trusting, they ate the fruit, and Satan's true character emerged.

He mixes truth with lies to deceive us. His temptations sound so real…so logical. We easily slip upon them. "Eat the fruit. You won't die." It was true. They would not die that day. However, their action would lead to eventual death over time. Satan lies. We suffer.

"You are weak," he whispers. "You are worthless. Just give up. You deserve this. You brought it upon yourself. You can't win. You'll end up alone. The pain never ends. This is it. This is all you get—one life, one death, and a heaping plate of suffering. You better toughen up. You better fight back, or figure out a way to distract yourself from the pain. That's the only way you'll survive."

Shortly after the juice from the fruit dried on their lips, God returned to Eden. He discovered his beautiful, innocent creation transformed. They became like angels in a singular way—knowing good and evil. What a sad day for God. If an angel could fall, could embrace evil as Satan had, how could God blindly afford all of humanity eternal life? Time proves well, many of us prefer darkness to light. An action like that would put the entire universe at risk.

God had no choice but to set them outside the garden, but before he did, God sat down beside Eve and prepared her for what was to come. He explained mortality and the pain of childbirth—things she knew nothing about. He spoke to Adam. Producing food would not happen as it did in Eden, when God simply thought a tree into being. "Outside," he told Adam, "you will have to force the earth to yield."

Then God made clothing from animal skin and wrapped it around them. He walked them to the gate and out into the wilderness. I often wonder, did God cry? Did he mourn like a parent watching his child suffer? One thing I know for certain is this. We cry. We live and we die. We return to the base element from which we were created: earth, dirt. How we live our lives reveals our hearts. Are we deceived, or are we fearless? Do we believe the lies or do we live like bold and brave warriors immersed in a very real battle for our souls? Do we let the snake's hiss kiss our ears, or do we flee from him?

Anastasia stopped there. She stared at the paper for a long while before looking up at her fellow writers. They watched her closely. One woman in the far corner broke the silence.

"I believed the lie," she said quietly. "I spent the last ten years watching my son drink himself to death. I accepted I could not change it. I threw my hands in the air and suffered quietly alone."

She whimpered. "But I realize now, I do not have to go down quietly. Even the problems far beyond our reach come from Satan. That's what you're saying right? Our pain, our suffering, and our fears—they all stem from him. My counteract will be simple. I'm going to get on my knees every morning and I'm going to pray to my God to keep my eyes open to the truth. I'll pray for Johnny, too. I can achieve peace through all this; maybe even joy."

Another woman who had lost her only son in Iraq turned her head and looked Anastasia directly in the face. "I believed it too. When my Cal died, I prepared myself to join him. 'God's will. God's will,' everyone kept saying. No, this world is Satan's will. Satan caused our pain. He caused us to fall—and all the bad things that happen to us happen because of him. They're not tests from God. I have hope, because I know God takes us back. My Cal is waiting for me, and no lie is going to keep me from him."

While emotions ran high that night, the group finished up with a few more pieces before retiring. On the long, dark drive home Anastasia thought of the two women who had shared their feelings. Pain comes at any age, she recognized. It wasn't unique to teenagers like Ellie. It comforted Anastasia to know she could share that pain with others. As believers, they did not have to go it alone. She looked forward to talking more with Ellie.

SALVAGED AND REPURPOSED

The following Tuesday was a typical day at work for Anastasia. Meetings and office tasks filled the morning hours. Right on time, her stomach turned inside out with hunger. At 11:30 a.m. she ran down to a quaint restaurant on Main Street and ordered a turkey, apple, and brie sandwich. She grabbed a milk jug out of the small refrigerator and paid the cashier.

It was an unusually warm fall day. The sun glistened off the dark green grass behind her building. A picnic table tucked beneath a set of Oak trees sat vacant. Anastasia spread her lunch out before her and let the rays of sun coming down through the branches warm her face and arms.

As she ate her food, she watched a young college student walk across the field to the sidewalk, toward the campus quad. It reminded her of her own days as a student. She had been through so much during those years and she survived it all. If she shared the next part of the story with Ellie, maybe it could give her daughter some hope and answers to why anger may not be the best choice. She began to write.

Dear Ellie,

The last months of senior year in high school were a blur of parties and late night walks along the streets alone. I had become more depressed than ever in those months, alienating most of my friends. I began frequently smoking pot all by myself. Between classes or during free periods I would hide in a doorway in a secluded hall and read rather than visit and hang out with friends. Someone must have turned me in out of fear I might hurt myself, because one afternoon the loudspeaker in my classroom blared, "Please send Anastasia Holton to the guidance counselor's office."

I dragged my feet all the way there, wondering what in the world they wanted with me. I had been in that office maybe five times in the last four years for standard meetings. The counselor quickly got to the point. "Some of the other students are concerned for you, Anastasia. They say you haven't been showering or changing your clothes and that you are very quiet all of the time. Is there anything you want to talk about?"

I almost wished someone had asked me that question five years before. Then I might have told them. Maybe if they had noticed I started dressing differently, hanging out more exclusively with a troubled crowd, and studying less, they could have saved me from myself. Now it was much too late. I had piled up my sin in giant heaps. It was too shameful. Once I might have been able to explain the hurt perpetrated on me by Reece and others like him. Now I had colored outside the lines for far too long, and I could blame it on no one but myself.

"No, I'm fine, Mrs. Palto. I'm just working through some stuff on my own. It's no big deal. Nothing to worry about, really," I answered.

Mrs. Palto went on, "Well, okay, but if you need to talk about anything—I mean anything—I'm here. Just stop by. Now I want to talk to you about something else. Anastasia, I want you to apply for college. Don't look so surprised! You are a really smart girl. Looking through your files from middle school until now, sure your grades have dropped, but you have real potential. I think life has gotten in the way, but you deserve a chance. Here, fill out this application. The school is really close by, in case you are worried about the change. When you are done, check this box. This is a special program for students like you, Anastasia. Your SAT scores would not get you into college, but you display potential and real intelligence. Being from a low-income family qualifies you for this assistance, and the program will provide extra preparation for college, so you're not behind right from the start. If you are accepted, it means you could go to college taking out minimal loans and earn a degree. You can have a chance for a better life. Get these papers back to me by Wednesday."

I barely heard a word Mrs. Palto said, but later I would be able to recall the conversation exactly. What would hit home later in life were the words my guidance counselor used: smart, potential, intelligent, a better life. It would take years for those words to sink in and for me to believe them. All I could do in that moment was take the paperwork and fill it out. I checked the box like I was told. I had no plans whatsoever, couldn't even remember the career fairs, college fairs, and planning sessions that had flooded most of the senior's lives that year. "How come I don't remember any of that," I wondered. I suppose, up until then, my life did not matter, even to me.

Within a month or so, I received a letter from the college. I pulled it out slowly, uncertain how to feel. "You have been accepted," it declared, punctuated by an unusually happy-looking exclamation point. I would be enrolled in a six-week preparatory program to get me ready for freshman year. I would be with a dozen other young people from similar backgrounds. We would become lifelong friends, survivors who unknowingly checked a box that would forever change our future.

My parents were more excited than I was. Just days before I left for college, I came home to find that my father had thrown away almost all of my clothes. I was irate. "This is a big chance, baby," my dad announced. "I'm sorry if you are angry with me, but I had to do it. This is a new start. Do you really want all of those professors to see you that way, wearing all those ripped up jeans and black t-shirts? Do you want to make that kind of first-impression?"

To be honest, I had not even thought of impressions or professors. I had been partying with a vengeance and, frankly, had completely forgotten college was coming. In fact, I had gotten so wasted the night before, some old dude and I smashed every piece of glass in his apartment. He was off his rocker. When he picked up the coffee pot and hurled it against the kitchen wall, it startled me. The glass exploded, and he laughed so loudly the neighbors called 911. Then he handed me the blender. It was a huge release to see all that stuff explode against the wall. Now, here I was, getting a lecture from my dad about my clothes and the future and people caring. For some unknown reason, he got my attention.

"Recreate myself," I thought. "That could be interesting. Imagine no one knowing me, knowing my past."

My mom took me shopping and bought me a few pairs of jeans, sweaters, and some black suede boots. They were cute; I actually looked cute. Somewhere, from way deep down inside, a tiny pocket of hope erupted and swirled up through my chest. I pushed it back down quickly, but there it was—a resurgence. My spirit said, "You can do this. This is your second chance, babe. Don't be so naive this time."

The first year of college went quite well. I remember lying on the couch after freshman year watching a television show on repurposing metal remnants found in farmyards and barns. The designer polished up an old round rusty piece of metal and crafted it into a chandelier. Before the shop even opened the following day, a customer knocked and knocked and knocked. The designer stumbled to the picture window, not yet filled up on caffeine, and asked, "Can I help you?" The passerby had seen the piece hanging inside and wanted to buy it right then, on the spot.

"Why do you enjoy this work so much?" a fellow designer asked her at the end of the show. She replied, "I like to take something that looks to everyone else like junk and get a vision for what it can be. Working through the process to that vision is like creating a master artwork. In the end, the piece is much more valuable than some shiny, sparkly thing from the shelf at the department store. It has a story, a life. It means something to the person who buys it and to the one who lets it go."

I felt my chest clench. "That's you," my mind whispered, "repurposed metal." Perhaps I too had a story; perhaps I was working through a process. I suddenly felt anxious for a vision of the final piece but nothing came. "In time," I thought. "In time."

College was good for me. It helped me discover my gifts—gifts that always existed but that I had not been fully aware of. I loved to write. As a little girl I would barricade myself in the back of the deep closet in my brother's room. I would stack a bunch of boxes, toys, and books into a makeshift wall, creating a little hidden cave in the corner where I could hide. I would pull out a flashlight, turn it on, and pick up a piece of paper and a pen. My fingers ached for the pen, and I never resisted its calling. I would write letters to my pen pals and friends who lived far away. I wrote stories about things I wanted to do or see. I even wrote descriptions of the things around me; those were my parents' favorites. They would read my stories about the closet and laugh out loud.

As a teen I wrote darker pieces, mostly poems. They were private, and I kept them hidden in a journal I tucked away in my backpack or under my mattress. College allowed me to grow my writing abilities. I studied journalism and loved the challenge of writing for assignments. I worked harder than I had at anything else in my life up to that point.

An experience emerged during those years similar to the one I had with my guidance counselor. One professor in particular saw a spark in me that I myself could not see. Anytime a new professor arrived or an alumnus of the college crossed our path, he would introduce me as "his best student." I blushed profusely at first, not accustomed to such attention.

He became angry with me when I failed to work to my potential. One particular day, after skipping a couple classes, he pulled me from the group and marched me out the back door straight into a snowstorm. He proceeded to shake his finger at me and make booming demands. "Straighten out. Get to class on time. No exceptions or you will fail!" That was all it took. I never missed his class again.

Another time, I took a semester off to earn some money. He tracked me down at my job and insisted on knowing my re-start date. For someone to believe in me like that shook my world up. "If they care," my mind whispered, "you better care." Another pocket of hope burst open, but I quickly pushed it back down.

College brought other discoveries too, some not as uplifting. I learned that those old deceptions buried deep in my heart still thrived. At dances, when aggressive boys pushed me out on the floor and held me too close, I remained silent. When people tempted me with alcohol, it went down way too smooth. After a long night of drinking, I generally did degrading things that I regretted after the haze wore off. I may have begun to believe in myself, but I still had little strength against the lie that said, "You are nothing. You deserve little more than a smirk, no matter how much of yourself you give. You'll always end up on the floor, picking up your books, while better girls get everything their hearts' desire. Quit trying, stupid girl."

I did discover one, fairly easy defense mechanism, though. Having a steady boyfriend allowed me a degree of protection. He would set boundaries like no drinking, no smoking, and no flirting. He would give ultimatums: "It's the drugs or me." He would step in if a guy got out of line with me. I could not be strong enough for myself, but he could. The only problem with that kind of solution is that I never learned to be strong for myself, to value my own life and body. So when he wasn't there, that same old lie came calling. The relationship came to a difficult end. It was inevitable. I could never give someone all they needed when my own needs died silently in my head. I had to discover my own strength.

The bell tower on Anastasia's building rang on the hour. One o'clock. Her lunch had ended a half hour before. She slid the paper into her purse and jogged inside.

RELAPSE

Anastasia's cell phone sat on her desk back in the office. An alert signaled a voicemail waiting. Anastasia punched in the password and listened.

"Mrs. Holton, this is Leann Jelsing. I don't know how to say this. I'm...I'm worried about Ellie. We... well...we left school today. Mrs. Holton, Ellie took some pills. She started acting really drowsy and disappeared. I'm afraid something might happen to her. Please call me. Or just come here." A loud click ended the message.

Anastasia's stomach twisted and heaved. She choked down a surge of vomit. Her heart raced as adrenaline pumped through her bloodstream. Her brain suddenly felt like a pressure cooker as thoughts steamed inside her head. The room became a bowl of swirling colors. She grabbed ahold of her chair to steady herself and blinked away the dizziness.

Anastasia snatched her purse from the floor and ran out of her office to the car. The race was on. She wondered who would reach the finish line first—her or some drugged up teenage boy with ill intentions. Anastasia began to cry.

Her tires screeched, marking the pavement in blackish-gray lines as she forced it to stop in front of Leann's house. "Get in," she shouted to the blonde girl on the dilapidated front porch.

Anastasia did not know Leann very well. She and Ellie recently began talking. They texted and hung out in school. Anastasia intended to take the girls out to lunch on Saturday to get to know Leann better and broach the topic of meeting her parents. You could never be too cautious about your kids' friends, and yet Anastasia remembered feeling elated that Ellie found a friend at all. Now it was too late for that. Leann must have sucked Ellie into this mess.

"What the hell happened, Leann? What did you girls get into?" Anastasia asked.

"Me?" Leann said, obviously astonished. "I didn't get into anything, Mrs. Holton, and frankly, I'm offended you would make that accusation." She pulled the door handle, ready to jump out of the car. Her tone was serious.

"I'm sorry," Anastasia spoke softly. "I just assumed."

"Well, don't assume," Leann snapped. "I'm not like that. I might come from the other side of town, but I'm a good person. Ellie talked *me* into skipping. I knew it was a really bad idea, but I had a feeling something might happen and I didn't want her to go with those guys alone. Turns out I was right."

"Who are these guys?" Tears welled up in Anastasia's eyes again.

Leann's tone softened. "They are juniors. They offered Ellie something to 'take the edge off.' She got in a big fight with that girl she used to be friends with. They were alone in the bathroom, and Ellie tried talking to her. She wanted to resolve it. She was trying to be nice. Well, that girl said some really rude things about Ellie being a loser and not talking to her ever again. Ellie didn't like that. She followed her out into the hall." Leann's voice trailed off.

"Leann, what happened between Ellie and Cassie?" Anastasia asked.

"It was pretty ugly, Mrs. Holton. Ellie said something like, 'What happened to you. You used to be a decent person; now you're just like them.' Cassie didn't go for it. She pushed Ellie really hard against a locker. Ellie turned red, and that was the end of it. She swung and hit Cassie right in the face. Cassie went down crying, and blood was coming out of her nose. Ellie called her a worthless bitch and took off running, right out of school. I followed her. The guys saw what happened and eventually wandered outside too. I was out behind the school trying to calm Ellie down. The guys came over and offered to help her feel 'chill.' Like I said, I didn't want her to go alone."

"Leann, thank you. You did the right thing calling me. I am so, so sorry you got mixed up in this, and I'm sorry I made assumptions. I will make sure that you don't get in trouble with the school or with your parents. Ellie, on the other hand…where do you think I can find her?"

Leann sighed. "Well, we were outside of the sub shop downtown when Ellie took the pills. I tried talking her out of it. We walked around for a while, and she started acting really funny. I knew she was pretty high, so I just kept following the boys. We were beside the library when one of the guys pulled a bunch of drawings out of his book bag and started showing them to me. I think he was distracting me on purpose. I turned around, and Ellie and the other guy were gone. I have no idea where they went, but I know where Jonathon lives. That's the guy I was talking to."

"Take me there," Anastasia demanded. They drove a little too fast, swerving around parked cars along side streets until they pulled up in front of an olive green apartment building. Anastasia saw overgrown bushes and garbage bags piled up at the corner of the side porch. Anastasia jumped from the car. "Stay here," she said to Leann. "I'll be right back."

Anastasia pounded on the front door until the glass in the old square panes shook. "Jesus," she heard someone snort inside. "I'm coming."

A heavy-set woman in her mid-fifties answered the door. She smelled of cigarettes and looked very upset to have been interrupted. A talk show blared in the background.

"I'm looking for Jonathon Clancy. Where is he?" Anastasia asked.

"What the hell do you want my son for?" she asked, squinting her eyes. "My daughter was with him about an hour ago, and now she's missing. You tell me where he is right now, or I'm calling the cops and we'll talk to them about it."

The woman's eyes widened. Anastasia thought she smelled marijuana.

The woman didn't want any trouble. "Jonathon, get your ass down here now," she yelled. "There's a lady who wants to talk to you. What the hell did you do this time?"

A teenage boy rounded the corner, shoving his hair out of his face as he stared at Anastasia. This boy was experienced. She recognized it right away. She had to be direct. She stared into his eyes for an extra second before she began, her fury bubbling just below their surface.

"Jonathon, if my daughter gets raped by your friend while she's high on pills, I am going to bring the police down on him and on you, do you understand," she said.

His eyes widened as he snapped a quick look at his mom before focusing back on Anastasia. "You distracted Leann while your little buddy took my daughter somewhere. I'll make sure you both end up in a juvenile facility. This is serious. Do you understand me? You have exactly five seconds to tell me where I can find Ellie or I'm dialing 911." Anastasia pulled her cell phone from her pants pocket.

The boy cracked. "Wait a minute. Just wait! They are in a blue-and-white house on Green Street between Second and Third. You can't miss it. There is a pickup truck in the driveway. Look lady, this isn't my fault. I don't want to be involved in this."

"You are involved," Anastasia snapped, her voice getting louder as her emotions spilled out. "You got involved when you decided it was okay to help your buddy get my daughter high and take advantage of her. You better hope that nothing has happened because if it has…"

Tears filled his eyes. Anastasia stopped yelling. She stared at him, suddenly caught off guard.

He looked so weak in that moment. His eyes glistened, but he choked back the feelings, enduring the barrage of curse words coming out of his mother's mouth in between gurgling, coughing spells. Anastasia realized he was a victim too, in another way, a child living amongst brokenness. Her heart swelled with pity for just a moment.

She spun around and raced to the car. The drive to Green Street was like those seconds before an accident, when you know your car is about to hit something and there is absolutely nothing you can do about it. You can't stop. You can't swerve. You hold on for dear life and pray that your car and your body are not torn apart upon impact. Time slows to a crawl. The sound of air exiting your lungs fills the silence around you. Your heart pounds against your own flesh. Bile fills your throat as the world in front of your windshield moves in scenes, independent of one another. Anastasia tried breathing in and out to stop the panic, but nothing worked this time. Her body entered survival mode.

The road acted like the last line of defense for this boy. Potholes jerked the girls back and forth inside the car. The narrow passage between parking on either side of the street slowed her to twenty-five miles per hour. She looked from side to side for the house, the truck.

"There it is," Leann shouted. "Right there, Mrs. Holton."

Anastasia pulled slowly into the driveway, her mind reeling with what she might find. This was a fairly rough neighborhood, one Anastasia herself had spent a lot of time in during her younger years. She could find just about anything in that house. Drugs. A weapon. Men with ill intent. Drugged-up women. Dealers. It was dangerous, but Anastasia's baby girl was inside that house and that life meant everything to her. She handed the keys and her cell phone to Leann.

"If something bad happens, get out of here and call the police, Leann. Do you understand me?"

"Yes ma'am," she said, "I understand."

"You did a good job, honey. I am very proud of you," Anastasia touched Leann's hand and then leaped out of the car. She didn't even knock. Anastasia walked quietly through the front door of the house. It was a dangerous move, but in the moment all that mattered was Ellie's safety, her dignity, and her innocence. Anastasia could not protect herself when she was a young girl, but she would fight to the death to protect Ellie.

What she found sickened Anastasia. This was a party house. She knew the kind. Likely, one or two strung-out adults lived there. They worked minimally and sold weed on the side to get by. They probably had several children but custody of none of them. They barely maintained the place. It stunk of beer and marijuana. The carpets were dirty. A low coffee table sat in front of a couch that maybe had been blue but now looked grayish. The table was strewn with ashtrays spilling over with butts, empty cans and bottles, and some dirt-covered playing cards. The teens—their most faithful regulars—likely came and went as they pleased because they brought business. In this boy's case, he must be a family member, because he had access when they were away.

Anastasia walked slowly and quietly down the narrow, dark hallway looking left to right at the rooms. First she passed a kitchen and small dining area. It stunk of old food. A solitary lamp light on the old wooden table cast shadows over dirty plates and more ashtrays. On the left, a bathroom door stood ajar. Finally, three doors ended the hallway – one directly in front of her and one on either side. "This is it," she whispered, "You can do this, Anastasia."

She listened as quietly as she could, holding her breath as her ears searched for sounds. A whimper came from the door in front of her, then she heard a deeper voice saying, "It's okay. Shhhhhhhh."

Anastasia burst into motion. He heart pounded harder than ever before. The pulsing turned into throbbing. She could taste it in her throat. She threw open the door and shouted, "Ellie," with all the power in her lungs.

The boy leaped from the bed, terrified, and fell hard against the wall. He had no shirt on, and his sixteen-year-old body was lean and sweaty. He looked like an animal about to become road kill. She remembered this kid. Her friend Julia knew his family. Eric had been raised by his aunt and uncle, but they weren't much better than his own parents. He grew up around drugs and alcohol. His own father had been jailed for molestation. It seemed Eric was doomed before his life began.

Ellie didn't move. Her body lay limp on the bed. Muffled sounds emerged, but only senseless gibberish.

"Ellie," Anastasia shrieked again. Nothing. Anastasia ran to her daughter's side. Ellie was dressed, but Eric had gotten as far as pulling down her zipper and lifting her t-shirt up over her bra. It was still around her neck. Anastasia pulled it down, covering Ellie's stomach. She zipped her pants and reached her hand underneath Ellie's neck, lifting up her head.

"Mom," Ellie slurred. "You saved me." A tear slipped down her cheek, and she passed out.

For the next hour, Anastasia felt like an actress in an action movie. Police sirens accompanied the ambulance. EMTs burst on scene, checking all of Ellie's vitals. They checked her pupils, her heart beat, her breathing, all while they loaded her onto the stretcher and into the ambulance.

The police asked lots of questions. Anastasia, Leann, and Eric gave their answers. All the stories matched. Eric knew he was in big trouble and almost seemed relieved, giving himself over to the process without any fight at all. The police picked up Jonathon for questioning too. It would be a long road for everyone involved—including Ellie. She would have to answer for attacking Cassie back at school and for taking pills, but now she was safe inside the ambulance, surrounded by medical staff.

Anastasia took a deep breath after the police cleared out and collapsed into her car. The cops had given Leann a ride home, and she was alone for a moment. Anastasia cried. Her whole life, it seemed, came spilling out at that moment. Every pain, every fear, every hidden secret and lie—it all came out. She was that thirteen-year-old girl in the basement, only this time, she stood up to Reece. She fought back. Not out of anger; she simply fought for what was right. As she sobbed into the steering wheel, her soul poured out the last bit of darkness that had taken root inside her so many years before. She prayed, thanking God for the phone call, for Leann, and for a chance to stop Ellie's mistake before it could grind its way into her heart. She prayed and prayed and prayed until she felt strong enough to start the car and make her way to the hospital. She would call Aaron on the way and tell him the whole story. They were likely in for a long and sleepless night.

GENTLE AS THE WIND

Hospital room 305 overlooked the river, which lined the north end of town where Anastasia grew up.

Staring out in the darkness—the bright lights of houses shimmered back at her. Anastasia let the memories flood in. She could see her first apartment. She could see the house she grew up in and the elementary school where she had enjoyed good friends. The parks where she played. The streets she had walked. The laughter and the loneliness.

Anastasia turned and looked at her daughter. Ellie slept deeply, the covers on the big hospital bed enveloping her. Her chest visibly rose and fell. Aaron snored in the reclining chair. Anastasia, on the other hand, could not sleep. She had been writing and reflecting so much lately, her brain buzzed. The upheaval with Ellie gave her the momentum she needed to finish what she began. She pulled out her paper and pen and started writing.

Dear Ellie,

College ended and I walked proudly across the stage in my cap and gown. My family came to congratulate me. I beamed. We held a small luncheon for a few close friends, professors, and mentors at my parents' house. It was a joyous day. Everyone hugged me and spoke words of praise. My news writing professor left me a little note that simply said, "Remember me when." Somehow…some way…I believed what he implied – that I had a future. That voice inside said, "You can do it, kiddo. You'll get there. You are going to accomplish something amazing."

For four years I had studied spirituality, world religions, philosophy, and all kinds of theories—and I found wisdom in all of them. That night, though, I kneeled down on the floor, leaned on my bed with my hands poised in prayer, and let go. It was the most base form of spiritual activity I ever engaged in. It reminded me of being a little girl with big blue eyes and long blonde hair, tucked up to my neck in a big comforter. My mom sat on the edge of my bed and placed my hands together. She taught me the Lord's Prayer. Word by word and line by line, Mom explained its meaning. I had said that prayer every single night of my life up until Reece. Suddenly, I could say it again for the very first time as an adult. I dared to believe God could deliver me.

I remember reeling in the irony of it all. That was the very bed I prayed in as a little girl, the same bed I returned to after the crushing blow Reece delivered in eighth grade. It was the bed where I had cut myself and cried violently until my body fell limp in sleep. There I was again as I spoke to God, asking for his direction.

"Lord," I whispered out loud, "help me. I want to change. I want to be strong. I want to stand up for myself and stop making bad choices. God, I give my life to you. Please. Please, make me whole." Something inside me stirred wildly that night. I cried a different cry. It cleansed me. I pulled out my old beat-up journal full of dark and stormy words, and I wrote something entirely different. The poem reflected my pain, but it also captured new hope. It did not deny who I had been, but it looked forward to something more. I titled the poem "Helen's Horizon," thinking of the pain and torment, the joy and love and loss that Helen of Troy must have endured. I thought of myself.

> She runs wild like the sea
> but gentle as the wind
> that picks the leaves off fallen trees
> and carries them again.

—

> The depth of her beauty
> can be seen in her eyes
> when lights catch tears swelling
> and she turns, and she hides.

—

> Like a dandelion she perseveres
> with an unassuming air.

PAMELA H. WITTER

Stunningly natural, her beauty flows forth
in blonde brush strokes of hair.

―

Sometimes she sits and watches the river
from her spot underneath the bridge.
She dreams of dropping down into the current
and swimming away like a fish.

―

But soon the church bells chime six o'clock
and she climbs down off the rocks.
She breathes in deep, exhales out
and begins her evening walk.

―

Ahead, a green carpet of trees
rolls on and on, consistently
seaming together with the soft, blue sky—
a quilted emblem for the truths in life.

―

Her eyes gleam.
She follows blue horizon dreams.

HOPE RISING

I felt a way to turn all that pain into something beautiful. After the poem was finished, I pulled the covers up to my chin and turned over. Little did I know that God had already formulated a plan for me.

Anastasia decided to save the ending. She took her other writings, added this new one, and tucked them away in an envelope. She put them in Ellie's purse along with a note that said, "We are taking a few days off for a little mother-daughter road trip. We should have done this a long time ago. I love you, honey."

PAVEMENT AND PURPOSE

The sun shone brightly through the car windows. A crisp blue sky exploded above. While the air was still cold on the skin, one could be convinced it was summer when the windows were up. Warmth filled the car. Ellie sat beside Anastasia, bags under her eyes. It had only been forty-eight hours since her mom tore through that bedroom door. She was mentally and physically broken. Leann had called Anastasia's cell phone six times since they parted company outside the dirty apartment where they found Ellie. She clearly cared deeply about her friend. Anastasia praised Leann's quick thinking when she spoke to her parents. They were proud of their daughter. Because of Leann's quick action,

Ellie's innocence was intact. For that, Anastasia was eternally grateful. The girls had not spoken since that afternoon. Ellie wasn't ready for human interaction just yet. She was in recovery, still trying to process everything that had happened to her.

The long drive to central Pennsylvania included dozens of postcard-esque views. They passed tree-lined roadways, expansive hilltops, and breathtaking valleys. All the while, Ellie slept. Anastasia breathed her in. Her little girl had grown so much, but remained her heart's purpose. She loved her daughter and to have this moment together—where she continued to care for and develop Ellie—brought both joy and responsibility to Anastasia's life.

After six hours of driving, Anastasia pulled into the parking lot of a small, single-level hotel. She walked inside and registered for a single room with two queen-sized beds, while Ellie slept in the car. Keys in hand, she carried their overnight bags to the room, and then returned to the vehicle. As she pulled back out of the parking lot and rounded the corner, heading toward the middle of town, Ellie stirred.

"Mom, where are we? How long have I been sleeping?" she asked.

"You have been sleeping for six hours, sweetie," Anastasia replied. "It's okay, you needed it. We are in the town where your dad and I met. I want to show you some things."

"I'm hungry. Can we get something to eat?" Ellie asked.

"That's perfect," Anastasia answered. "That's exactly what we'll do." She thought, "And that's where I'll start the story."

Anastasia pulled into the parking lot of a small diner tucked away on a side street off the main drag. Aunt Pat's Place, the sign read. It was just hidden enough for Ellie. She wouldn't want to be around a lot of people right now. It was an old building, with lots of wear and tear, but it was loved. Pictures of local sports teams and country fairs covered the walls. There were signed dollar bills in frames near the cash register. Behind the stool-lined counter hung a picture of Aunt Pat—a big lady in a plaid, button shirt and a cowboy hat, with a large, toothy smile. The girls sat at a booth in the back corner and looked over the menu.

Suddenly a voice called out, "Anny!" in a near-shriek from behind the counter. Ellie didn't even lift her head. She never heard her mother called that, but Anastasia knew the voice right away. Frankly, she was shocked that anyone she knew was still working at the diner.

She lifted her head and smiled broadly at Jessie. Jessie had been Anastasia's dear friend all those years ago—two girls trying to make sense out of life. Jessie saw Anastasia through some real turmoil. Here she was, nearly fifty years old, still waiting tables. Jessie looked great. Her tall frame floated effortlessly across the floor.

Anastasia jumped from her seat. She wrapped her arms around Jessie and squeezed. Jessie laughed that same old laugh—a gut-level laugh, the kind that made everyone in earshot happy. That's when Ellie looked up, quizzically.

Jessie did not hesitate. "Oh my *God*, Anastasia, is this your daughter? She looks just like you! Oh Lord, get up and give me a hug, dear! I can't believe this." Jessie didn't give Ellie time to move. She swept Ellie out of her seat and squeezed her breathless.

Ellie cracked a small smile. She tried to hide it, but Jessie brought that out in people. Ellie couldn't resist her charm.

After introductions and a disguised explanation of their mother-daughter trip, Jessie took the girls' orders and disappeared into the kitchen with a promise from Anastasia they would talk more, later; maybe meet up for coffee after closing.

Anastasia and Ellie settled into the booth as they awaited their food. Neither spoke at first. After a few minutes, Ellie looked up at her mom.

"Thank you," she whispered.

"Ellie, you don't have to," Anastasia began, but Ellie interrupted.

"Mom, I do. I'm…ashamed of myself." She started to cry softly. "Ellie, listen to me now. Do not go there. You are dealing with some deep feelings right now, and you are trying to understand a world that hurts. You made a mistake, but you know what? You are okay. Today—right now—you are safe. That is an immense blessing. Do you know that? You have an opportunity here that most young ladies in your position never do. You gained wisdom without the full impact of pain. I don't want you to apologize or feel guilty. I want you do something about it."

Anastasia spoke those last words with more intensity than she had used with her daughter in a long, long time. Ellie noticed. She didn't dare break her mother's gaze. "What are we doing here, Mom?" she asked.

"Ellie, I used to work here," Anastasia said.

"What?"

"Yup, I worked here. I had just finished college and had applied for a bunch of jobs at newspapers all throughout New York and Pennsylvania. It was a tough economy, and there were few jobs to be had. I got a part-time job as a reporter for a paper here. It was a start, and I knew it would lead to more opportunities later, but it didn't pay the bills. I needed to supplement, so I took a job at the diner to make ends meet. I loved it so much! For the first time in my life, I was independent. I was poor, but that didn't matter. I was doing it on my own. I had a little apartment a couple blocks away. I'll show it to you. Jessie and I were good friends. She lived upstairs from me and got me the diner job. I had never waited tables before, but Aunt Pat gave me the job on Jessie's recommendation. I picked up waitressing quickly." Anastasia laughed.

"Mom, I can't picture you working here," Ellie whispered.

"Well, you only know me as a business woman. There is a lot you don't know."

"Obviously," Ellie retorted, and then backtracked. "I didn't mean that how it sounded. I'm just learning a whole lot about you right now. I thought…I thought you were so…perfect."

Anastasia laughed out loud. "Far from it, Ellie. I had a whole painful life before you came along. Believe it or not, I was young and crazy once. The thing is, I learned from my mistakes. I also found God along the way. Things changed then, but let's eat now. We'll talk more about all this later."

Ellie welcomed the silence. They ate quietly, enjoying being together. Ellie and Anastasia could be dead silent, and it wasn't awkward at all. They ate their greasy cheeseburgers on big white buns without any thought of carbs or fat calories. Anastasia usually watched her weight quite closely, but this was a welcome treat for both of them. They topped off their meals with gravy fries and Cokes, leaving crumbs all over the linoleum table. Despite the six hours of sleep Ellie enjoyed on the drive there, she looked like she could drift away at any moment. Her eyelids drooped, and her hair was a tangled mess. They ordered coffees to go before saying their goodbyes to Jessie.

Anastasia handed her friend a piece of paper before leaving. "Call me when your shift ends," it said. "If you're not busy; let's meet up at the hotel lobby. Lots to talk about." Jessie nodded.

The girls returned to the car. Anastasia slid the key into the ignition and turned it. The car rumbled to a start. Slowly she pressed her foot to the gas and began across the bumpy, rock-covered driveway. The car rocked as they crossed the threshold from the parking lot to the smooth street.

A flood of memories filled Anastasia's mind. The last time she pulled out of that parking lot, it was pitch black outside. That night, all those years ago, she didn't notice the man following behind her—the one who had been hiding behind the building next to the dumpster, the one she didn't see until it was much too late. Anastasia squeezed her eyes shut for a moment to expel the memories and the swelling emotions in her chest. She heard herself scream all those years ago; a scream that she would never forget.

SNAPSHOT MEMORIES

Ellie perked up after chugging a big cup of Aunt Pat's blacker-than-black coffee. No surprise there. Aunt Pat's coffee could wake the dead. Anastasia and Jessie used to say that if they ever needed a get-away car, they could take a cup of that coffee and start up the old, abandoned tractor in Jared Black's corn field.

"We called it liquid tar," Anastasia joked. They had been driving for about ten minutes toward the other end of town, away from the business district and the bustling afternoon crowd.

"Where are we going now, Mom?" Ellie asked.

"There," Anastasia said, pointing.

Ellie looked out of her window and her eyes opened wide. A beautiful cemetery splayed out before them, the most beautiful cemetery she'd ever seen. Dark green, perfectly manicured grass covered the ground everywhere. Many small hills mixed with areas of flat land, creating a sea of snapshots. A small lake could be seen in the center, surrounded by cement benches. Statuettes looked over the graves. Colorful flowers burst out of the ground in perfectly placed patches. The occasional small, square building stood erect—a family name engraved at the top, stained glass windows all the way around. Regularly placed water spigots made gardening easier for families and groundskeepers. The roadways throughout the cemetery curved and turned, creating maze after maze after maze.

"I would come here every single day, Mom," Ellie whispered.

"I did," Anastasia said. She drove to a back corner of the cemetery, an area void of visitors and full of very old-looking stones, before parking the car and inviting Ellie for a walk.

"Why here, Mom?" Ellie asked.

"This is where I met your dad," Anastasia answered.

"You met dad here?" Ellie asked, surprised.

"Yeah, right over there," Anastasia pointed.

Ellie's eyes found what must have been the most amazing grotto the world had ever seen. Stone stairways wound down from six different angles to an elegant flagstone floor below. Low English-looking rock walls created a circle from the top of each stairway to the next. Stone planters filled the inner walls with blasts of beautiful color and hanging ivy as the sun poured into the grotto from above. From the main staircase, a walkway of beautiful red rock cut through the flagstone floor and led to the focal point of the space—a huge statue of the Mother Mary with her arms outstretched. Ellie stared at the woman, feeling as if she could simply stand there and receive Mary's blessing.

"This is amazing, Mom," she said with an unwavering gaze.

"I know," Anastasia answered. "Here, sit down." They sat on one of the cement benches that lined the wall, leaning back as the sun tickled their skin. Anastasia began.

"Every day my shift at the newspaper ended at 3:00, barring some unexpected and newsworthy development. I usually had about an hour and a half before I had to be at the restaurant. I packed a late lunch and brought it here, where I would eat. My days were so busy and full of people, I really needed that time to unwind or I'd go crazy. The silence appealed to me. Few people come to this section of the cemetery, except the occasional wedding party. Even that was rare, though. This grotto is so far back in the cemetery, you have to know that it's here.

"It was a fall day. The leaves on the trees had fully changed and some had fallen. The grotto floor was sprinkled with dashes of yellow and orange. I brought a book that day, *The Art of Happiness*."

Ellie giggled.

"What?" Anastasia asked.

Ellie smiled. "Self-help, Mom."

"Hey, that's an awesome book," Anastasia said. "I was really struggling, Ellie. Do you know what I mean?"

Ellie's expression changed. Her eyes grew serious. She looked at her mother. "I do…now." "I was there," Anastasia continued. "I had always been a"—she searched for the right word—"a quiet girl, a timid girl. For some reason, my words always got trapped inside my head, and they could never escape. Something bad would be about to happen and I had all the words I needed right at the tip of my mind, words that would let me escape to a safe place, and I just froze. The words never came out, not until later. They sat there, stuck in time, watching me suffer over and over again. I had become so depressed, some days I wanted to die. Yet I had this inner strength. It kept saying, 'No! You aren't ready yet. You can do this.' But I had no idea how. The first step, I thought, was to get ahold of my emotions. If I could do that, I could practice being stronger. Speaking. That book really put me on the right path. It brought me inner peace I hadn't felt before. There was one serious problem with that, though." Anastasia paused for a long while. She was lost in a memory.

"Mom," Ellie nudged her. "Mom!"

Anastasia snapped back to the present. "I'm sorry," she said quietly.

"It's okay, Mom. What was the problem?"

Anastasia sighed deeply and looked up at the light blue sky. "The problem was that my weakness followed me. I was breaking free of some old chains and I was ready for healing, for renewal, and for a better life. But I had been friendly to a young man at the restaurant named Joey. He wasn't right. I knew that; but the old me never paid attention to any red flags. The old me stumbled forward and let anyone in, no matter how dangerous they were or how much damage they could cause. My mind whispered, 'don't,' but my body moved me forward silently.

"Joey had been coming in more and more frequently. He was young and cute, but very rough around the edges. He had issues, if you know what I mean. We had bumped into each other outside of the restaurant as well—shopping or going for a walk. We always stopped to talk. The talks got longer and longer. Joey shared some deep issues from his past. His father had been mentally ill, and in those days, they didn't have great treatment options. Joey lived through some atrocious abuse, the effects of which left him broken. His skinny frame and dark, scraggly hair revealed a young man full of pain. I didn't look beyond that. I felt sorry for him.

"Joey started following me. I didn't know it. I just noticed that he was around a lot. One day, outside of the bookstore downtown, Joey watched me through the big storefront windows. I saw him and assumed he had paused as he passed by. I waved and held up one finger, asking him to wait. On the sidewalk, he told me about his appointments and doctors' visit that day. He looked uncharacteristically happy.

"'What's up,' I asked him. 'Anny, I want to ask you a question,' he started slowly. 'Would you ever… would you…will you,' he stumbled.

'What is it, Joey?' I asked.

'Will you go to the movies with me tonight,' he finally blurted out.

"I was stunned. Honestly, I did not see him that way. He was Joey, you know? I did not want to go. My instincts told me not to do this, but the words got all jammed up in my head, and I couldn't bear to hurt his feelings. I said okay, but just as friends. I reiterated the 'just as friends' part twice more; but Joey's eyes sparkled as if he didn't hear me. My stomach turned.

"Later that night, after my shift ended at Aunt Pat's, I drove to the movie theater on Alena Drive. Joey stood outside the front doors. He was wearing his normal clothes—baggy jeans, sneakers and a t-shirt, but it looked like he had actually ironed the t-shirt. There were crisp lines where he pressed the sleeves. He still had dark circles around his eyes, and his teeth obviously had not been well-maintained over the years, but he smelled like soap and cologne and even had gel in his hair. I felt I had made a huge mistake. I insisted on buying my own ticket and popcorn, and the movie went by quickly. Outside, I asked Joey if he'd like a ride home. He accepted.

"Outside of the two-story, pale blue house where he lived with his grandmother, Joey sat still in his seat. 'Well, that was fun Joey, thanks for inviting me,' I said, hoping he'd remember the just friends thing, but he didn't. Joey quickly leaned over and put his lips on mine. I pulled back instinctively. 'Joey, just friends, remember,' I shouted.

"His eyes narrowed. He didn't believe me. He leaned in again, and I slapped his face. I shocked myself. I wasn't sure where this sudden burst of inner strength had come from. I had been reading that book—and others—and was beginning to make sense of my life. Maybe I was stronger than I thought I was. It was amazing. I suddenly felt like I could do or say anything! 'Get out,' I yelled at Joey.

"His eyes glared back at me, rage brewing behind them. 'You fucking tease,' he whispered, as he turned and got out of the car. I was so high on adrenaline that it didn't scare me. It should have. I should have been terrified."

Anastasia paused to look at Ellie. Her daughter sat, staring—completely still; her eyes wide open and mouth agape. Anastasia realized the story was just as terrifying to hear. She put her hand on Ellie's shoulder.

"Sweetie, its okay. I'm here, right? I must have survived that." Ellie blinked and let her shoulders slump just slightly. A tear slipped out. "There's more," Anastasia said. She didn't want Ellie to open the flood gates just yet. She wanted to tell her everything. She knew Ellie could relate to every word and every feeling. The fear. The strength. The darkness. The pain. They were on this journey together.

NEW BONDS

Anastasia continued her story. "The next day, after my shift at the paper, I came here. I was high on life, Ellie. Nothing could stop me. I felt exhilarated. I felt free for the first time in my life. After all those hurts from when I was young, I finally learned to speak. I stood up for myself, and I felt like superwoman. That night, I had dreamed bigger than I ever had. It was a beginning of the woman you see in me today—confident and strong and capable."

Anastasia stood up and walked to the statue of Mary. She made the sign of the cross and kissed her fingers gently. Ellie watched. She was seeing her mom in a whole new way, a woman who existed outside of their little world. She saw weakness she had never noticed before, and strength. She saw a human being. She saw brokenness, pain, and healing. She saw all kinds of depth in her mother's eyes.

Anastasia turned and lowered herself into a sitting position on the small ledge just below the statue. "I was sitting right here the next day, the day after Joey tried to kiss me and I slapped his face. I was seeing this grotto in a new light. I felt a spiritual presence."

A butterfly floated down into the grotto and passed Ellie's shoulder. Sporadic white clouds interrupted the blue carpet of sky above them. The sun glistened off Anastasia's light blonde hair.

"For the first time as a young woman, I considered all the implications of strength," Anastasia continued. "I didn't see a waitress and a part-time reporter in the mirror. I saw a woman who could run the entire newspaper. I saw a CEO, a mother, a wife, and a best friend. I remember looking up at Mary and thinking, 'This woman was blessed by God. She didn't deserve it. She had likely made mistakes. She was fearful, but God gave her a gift anyway. He entrusted her with his most precious thing—his son. He put Jesus in her care, supplied the faith she needed to take on the challenge, and set her free.' I thought, 'That's me. That's all women everywhere. God entrusts us with life, he equips us with the strength and faith we need, and he lets us go.' Ellie, we determine what we do with all of that. I had to love myself enough to see the possibilities. I needed to honor God's gift to me—the gift of my life."

"Mom." Ellie spoke softly. "How did you move beyond the pain? I am strong. I always have been. It is the pain that ruins me. I don't know what to do with it."

"Pain," Anastasia said aloud. "There is only one thing you *can* do with it. You give it to God. You let it go. By doing that, he heals you from the inside out. It doesn't mean you won't go through painful emotions or that you won't cry or scream out. It does, however, mean that you allow yourself to experience it without acting on it; unless acting on it means you do something positive."

"You build people up instead of tearing them down. God told us that the greatest commandment is to love. If you are not acting out of love, than you are only creating more pain in the world. That accomplishes nothing. If you allow yourself to feel the pain without wanting to hurt someone else, then you are destroying it. You are stopping it dead in its tracks. You are ending that particular cycle of hurt.

"On the other hand, if you react to your pain by seeking to destroy someone or something, you are giving that particular cycle of hurt the momentum to go on. It will grow and grow until one day, it becomes something awful. It becomes like Joey—incapable of seeing beyond itself. The best thing to do with pain is to feel it and let it go."

Anastasia stood up and walked to the top of the stairs on the east side of the grotto, the only area partially shaded by a huge oak tree. "Your dad was standing right here, Ellie, the first time I ever saw him." Ellie looked at her mother. She pictured her dad looking down at Anastasia, sitting on that little ledge in front of Mary.

"I was looking at Mary with the biggest smile on my face," Anastasia continued. "I can't imagine what your dad must have thought. All of a sudden I heard a deep, gentle voice say, 'You are awfully happy about that statue!'"

"I nearly leapt out of my skin," Anastasia said. "I fell off that little ledge and stumbled back a couple feet. My heart was pounding. Aaron ran down the steps, horrified that he'd startled me so badly. He steadied me and apologized profusely. I burst into laughter. He started to laugh too. That was when I noticed how handsome he was. He had soft brown hair that swept across his forehead. His pale brown eyes reminded me of milk chocolate. He had the most beautiful smile—radiant, joyful, and most of all, safe. I think I fell in love that very second.

"After several more apologies, he asked what I had been doing. I told him I was listening to Mary, that she had told me something I'd been waiting to hear for a very long time. He smiled and stuck out his hand. 'I'm Aaron,' he said. He was a young college graduate, having just completed trade school, and was apprenticing with a local contractor. I mentioned the newspaper and the restaurant. It was time for me to be at work, so I excused myself, and we went our separate ways. I had no idea at that moment I was looking at my lifelong partner. I had no idea I would see a lot more of Aaron. C'mon Ellie. I have another place to take you."

The girls climbed up the grotto stairs and made their way to the car.

Just before opening the passenger side door, Ellie paused. She looked back at the grotto. "Give me a minute, Mom."

Ellie turned and ran back. She climbed down the stairs and walked to the statue of Mary. She kneeled down on her knees, resting her elbows on the little stone ledge. She put her face in her hands and began to pray.

Anastasia could not remember a time when Ellie prayed as a teenager. It was beautiful and brought tears to her eyes. Anastasia pulled out her phone and snapped a picture of Ellie. She would show it to Aaron. This was as much his moment as anyone's. The sun began to set as the girls pulled away from the cemetery. Ellie's cheeks were flush from fatigue. The caffeine from Aunt Pat's coffee had worn off. Ellie's eyes drooped. Anastasia decided she would continue their talk the following day. For now, Ellie needed rest.

She pulled into the parking lot of the hotel and walked her daughter up the stairs to their room. Ellie sunk into the bed and escaped into the night. Anastasia lay down on her own bed. A few minutes later, Anastasia' telephone vibrated on the nightstand. "That must be Jessie calling," Anastasia thought.

The old friends met in the hotel lobby. Ellie was fast asleep upstairs, and Anastasia left a note for her. The next few hours flew by as Jessie and Anastasia reminisced about the old days. Anastasia filled her in on the activities of the past month. She brought her up to speed on the story, including their visit to the cemetery that day. Jessie leaned back in the tall, wingback hotel chair and sighed.

"Did you tell Ellie about what happened that night, after work?" Jessie asked, her eyebrows furrowed in a scowl. "No," Anastasia answered. She paused. "I want you to tell her that part."

Jessie's eyes widened. "What?" she asked, startled. "Why?"

"Jessie, I only remember bits and pieces. I won't do it justice and frankly, I don't know if I would make it through to the end. Will you do it? Will you tell her?"

"That was the craziest night of my entire life, Anny," Jessie said. "To this day it gives me shivers."

"I know, Jessie. I have only talked about it with my counselor and with God. Aaron and I barely speak of it." Anastasia looked down at the floor and shuffled her feet. "Ellie doesn't know. I didn't even tell my parents. They had to get the full story from the police." She paused before looking back up at Jessie, more serious now.

"Before Joey showed up that night, I had already decided I was going to change my life. I didn't know how. I simply knew good things were coming my way. I always thought of Joey's 'visit' as a blip, you know, an inconvenient interruption. I had started down a better path, and he was a delay. He slowed my progress, but he didn't stop me."

She paused. "Jessie," she said, looking straight into her friends eyes.

"What is it Anny?" Jessie asked.

"I'm sorry."

"Sorry for what?"

"I am sorry that I didn't stay in touch with you, that I didn't thank you. You and Aaron saved my life, and I didn't even say goodbye. I hope that you can forgive me for that. It has always haunted me. I…I just didn't know how to see you. I was afraid if I looked at you, I would never leave. I was afraid I would freeze. I loved you so much."

"Sweetie," Jessie said, reaching her hand out and resting it on Anastasia's knee, "you have nothing to apologize for. I know as well as anyone how to escape. I have been hiding in this place for twenty years. Maybe it is time I take a little road trip down memory lane myself. It could do me a lot of good. I love you, Anny. Always have. Always will. Somehow, I knew I would see you again, that you would come walking through that door one day. I knew that you would be amazing. Maybe all this time I have been waiting to see you, to make sure you were okay. Maybe I wanted proof that a person can suffer in this life and still thrive. You coming here has given me something I have not had since I was a little girl—faith. Faith in God. Faith in myself. Faith in life and in healing. The moment I saw you and your daughter sitting at that table, I heavy burden came off of me. Please don't apologize for that."

The ladies reached out for each other and hugged for a long time, tears streaming down both of their faces. Before heading home, Jessie made plans with Anastasia for the next day. They would meet at Jessie's apartment late morning, and they would finish what they had started all of those years ago. They would tell their story to a teenage girl desperately in need of hope and strength. They would do this together, for Ellie.

AWAKENING

The morning sun poured in the windows and showered Anastasia in warmth. Her body possessed an internal alarm clock. At 6:15 every morning, she woke up whether she had slept two hours or ten. This morning, the sunshine tickled her awake before her own body could accomplish the task. It was 6:10.

She stretched her legs until her feet poked out of the end of the bed, rubbed her eyes, and rolled over to look at Ellie in the bed on the other side of the room. The covers lay flat. The bed was empty. Anastasia rolled up on her side and threw the heavy comforter off.

"Ellie," she called as she walked toward the bathroom. Ellie was not there. Anastasia put on her sneakers, layered a sweater over her pajama top, picked up her purse, and headed out the door. She walked down the hallway toward the lobby. She glanced in to see if Ellie had taken early advantage of continental breakfast. Ellie was not there. She walked through the lobby and looked out the front door toward their car. No Ellie. She walked down the first-floor hallway toward the weight room and the pool. She didn't find Ellie anywhere. Anastasia began toward the elevators, concerned.

The housekeeper touched her elbow and asked, "Are you looking for the young lady?"

Anastasia nodded enthusiastically. The cleaning lady, whose nametag read Eva, smiled. "I saw her leave about twenty minutes ago. I had to take some garbage out to the dumpster and watched her walk to the park down the street. I bet you will find her there."

Anastasia thanked Eva profusely and wandered toward the park, still wearing her pajamas. Sure enough, Ellie was there, sitting underneath a beautiful old oak—much like the one in the cemetery. She had a book in her hand and was reading, pausing occasionally to look off into the distance. As she got closer, Anastasia noticed Ellie was holding a Bible.

She must have pulled it out of the nightstand at the hotel room. Anastasia walked up quietly and sat down beside Ellie.

"Whatcha doing?" she asked.

"Oh, hi, Mom," Ellie answered. "Just reading. I went to bed so early I was up by 4:30. I got bored sitting in the room. You were breathing so heavily, I didn't think you'd be up for a while, so I took a walk. Is that okay?"

"Of course, honey," Anastasia answered. "Did you read anything interesting in there?"

"Yeah. I did," Ellie said.

"Anything you want to share?" Anastasia asked.

"You know, I always thought this book was so ancient, so irrelevant. I still have a million questions, but I figured something out this morning, Mom."

"What did you figure out?" Anastasia asked softly.

"I remember reading the Bible in Sunday school. The stories seemed fantastical. Jonah living in the whale's belly—it was like a cartoon on TV. Once in a while something really connected though, like when Ms. Redmond would get all serious and ask us about our problems. The kids would share things like getting picked on at school, their parents' divorce, or getting beat up by their brother. Ms. Redmond would throw the lesson plan out, grab a board game to play, and talk to us. She always knew exactly what to say. She would find some verse that perfectly fit our problem—as if she knew the conversation ahead of time."

Anastasia watched her daughter talk and smiled.

Ellie continued. "She would make us write things down and put them in our pocket; or she would tell us to hang them on our bedroom wall. She wanted us to use the lesson when we needed it. One time she gave us these coins that said, 'Connected to the Vine.' She told us that we should carry the coin in our pocket. When we got really upset about something, we could rub the coin and remember we are always connected to God. Then we would know to pray at the very moment we had a problem and God could help us feel better or figure out a solution." Ellie smiled. "It really worked, Mom! Ms. Redmond said it was too easy to forget to invite God in when we were upset—even for adults. Is that true?" she asked.

Anastasia nodded her head.

"I never told you this, but I carried that coin in my pocket from third grade through sixth grade. It wasn't until middle school that I stopped. You know, I never once thought about it before, but things went downhill about the time I stopped carrying that coin, when I stopped praying." Ellie paused.

Anastasia touched her daughter's hand. "I knew you carried that coin, Ellie," she said. "Sometimes you would leave it in your pants pocket. I got in the habit of checking each night. If the coin was there, I put it on your nightstand. I was so proud of you for being faithful and trusting God. It made you stronger. I remember when you stopped carrying it, too. It broke my heart the day I found it, still sitting on your night stand after you had gone out to wait for the bus. At first I thought it was an accident, but the coin didn't move for an entire week.

"Seventh grade was one of your toughest years. I worried about you all the time. I prayed for you every day and still do. One of my prayers is that you find your way back. Life is not guaranteed to be easy, Ellie. In fact, you can almost count on it being hard, but you don't have to struggle through it alone." Anastasia touched the blue Bible on the ground next to Ellie. "Did you discover anything interesting?" she asked.

Ellie's smile grew. "Mom, what I found freaked me out a little bit. I carried this Bible out here, and on the way, I was thinking in my head, 'God, please help me make sense of all this. I am so confused.' I actually thought those words: make sense of this." Ellie laughed out loud. "I flipped the Bible open to the book of Ecclesiastes. I almost dropped it right on my foot. The first chapter was called 'Nothing Makes Sense.'" Ellie's eyes were wide. She looked at Anastasia. "Isn't that awesome!"

"Sometimes God works that way," Anastasia said, grinning. "Not always, but sometimes."

Ellie continued, "I thought, 'Okay, God, what do you want me to know?' I read the first five chapters. It was written by the King of Jerusalem. You'd think this guy should be happy. He had it all. He wasn't content, though. He was like, 'Nothing makes sense. People live and die. Life goes on. Everything is boring.' He said you can't really change anything. Even if you work hard, you're going to die and someone else will benefit from all your work. He tried to be really good and perfect. Then he decided to just have fun; but no matter what he did, he said it was like chasing the wind."

Ellie picked up the book and pushed through the pages. When she found the verse she was looking for she put her finger underneath it and read aloud.

> Then I decided to compare wisdom with foolishness and stupidity. And I discovered that wisdom is better than foolishness like light is better than darkness. Wisdom is like having two good eyes; foolishness leaves you in the dark.
>
> Ecclesiastes 2:12-14

She looked up from the book.

"But then the king said it *still* doesn't matter, because we all die anyway. I started getting annoyed, like geez, what a pessimist; but he is right. What's the point?" She looked back down. "He talks about all the pain and injustice, poverty and sin. It really bothered him. Then he said something else."

> Everything on earth has its own time and its own season. There is a time for birth and death, planting and reaping, for killing and healing, destroying and building, for crying and laughing, weeping and dancing, for throwing stones, embracing and parting. There is a time for finding and losing, keeping and giving, for tearing and sewing, listening and speaking. There is also a time for love and hate, for war and peace.
>
> Ecclesiastes 3:1-8

A tear trickled down Ellie's cheek. "Since life is full of all this good and bad, he said the best thing we can do is be happy. If we do the right things and get joy out of our work, God will give us wisdom and understanding, and that's better than foolishness. He said, 'You may be poor and young. But if you are wise, you are better off than a foolish old king who won't listen to advice.'"

She rubbed her eyes and started talking again, more slowly this time. "Then he said, 'You are better off to have a friend than to be all alone, because then you will get more enjoyment out of what you earn. If you fall, your friend can help you up. But if you fall without having a friend nearby….'" She struggled to finish. "'You are…you are really in trouble.'" With those last words, Ellie began to cry. Days' worth of tears fell from her eyes. She shook as all the pain of the past week poured out of her. Between her sobs she tried to speak but the words came out slow and difficult.

"You and Leann were my friends," she said, "even though I didn't deserve it. You came for me. I was so mean to you, Mom. And what if you hadn't come? I would be in real trouble now. It would be a lot harder to get through all this if you hadn't come when you did…and I would never take your advice." Her sobs overtook her words.

Anastasia wrapped her daughter up in her arms and squeezed her in close. "It's okay, baby," she said, "It's okay. I'm here now. I've got you."

They sat like that until Ellie breathed normally again, until she had no tears left to cry. Her eyes were surrounded by dark red, puffy circles, and her face was blotchy. Anastasia's hair was damp from Ellie's tears. She pushed her daughter upright and looked her in the face. "Ellie, the author of that book seemed pretty negative, huh, like there's no point to anything. Just find your happiness and trust God."

Ellie nodded.

"Well, there is a lot of truth in that. We need to find our inner peace; our joy. Trusting and following God will help us through our toughest times. There is more, though. Do you mind if I share my favorite verse with you?"

Ellie nodded again.

Anastasia turned to John 14:23 and read, "If anyone loves me they will obey me. Then my Father will love them, and we will come to them and live in them." She turned the page to John 15:7 and continued. "Stay joined to me and let my teachings become part of you. Then you can pray for whatever you want, and your prayer will be answered." Anastasia looked up at Ellie to explain. "Jesus was leaving behind the Holy Spirit to live in us since he was going back to heaven to be with God. He didn't want to leave us alone. When we connect with Jesus—like staying connected to the vine—and learn to follow him, our prayers will come from the right heart. Then our prayers will be heard; like your prayers when you were a little girl."

Ellie smiled.

"Sometimes we have to be really patient," Anastasia continued. "It can take time for God to work out our prayers, but I know from experience just how faithful He is to us." Anastasia reached down into her purse. She shuffled around the bottom until she found what she was looking for. She pulled her hand out, her fingers clenched around something. She turned her hand palm up and opened her fingers, revealing a little, round, silver coin. It read, "Connected to the Vine."

Ellie gasped. She reached out quickly and took the coin from her mother's hand. "How did you know to bring that, Mom?" She immediately recognized it as her own. It had the same little nick on the edge that it had when she carried it.

Anastasia laughed. "I didn't know to bring it," she said. "I have been carrying that coin in my purse for two years, praying for the right time when you would want it back. Why don't you keep it, Ellie. It's yours."

Ellie put the coin into her pants pocket and hugged her mother.

Anastasia continued, "There's just a bit more." She picked the Bible back up. "When you become fruitful disciples of mine, my Father will be honored. I have loved you, just as my Father has loved me. So remain faithful to my love for you." (John 15:8-9) Anastasia paused, moved her finger just slightly, and then continued, "I have told you this to make you as completely happy as I am. Now I tell you to love to each other, as I have loved you." (John 15:11-12)

"That was the greatest commandment, Ellie—to love God with all our hearts and to love our neighbor as ourselves. That is what it means to obey Jesus. It is so simple. Everything else flows from there—all the rules and commands follow the simple act of loving. By loving God and others—and by loving ourselves—God will live in us and we can lift our prayers up to him. We are never alone.

"Ellie," Anastasia said, "you may have stopped praying back in the seventh grade, but I never did. I always prayed for God to protect and keep you. That day, when you were in so much trouble, God answered *my* prayer. He used Leann to protect you."

Ellie leaned back into her mother, and they hugged for a long while. "Thanks, Mommy," she whispered in Anastasia's ear. "I love you." Eventually, the girls returned to the hotel. They showered and readied themselves for the day. They ate continental breakfast in the hotel lobby among a scattering of business people and young families on vacation or visiting family. By ten they had checked out and put their bags in the trunk.

"We are going to spend some time with Jessie this morning before we head home," Anastasia said as they turned out of the parking lot. She looked out of the window and drew in a long, deep breath. "We have one last thing to tell you about."

THE FINAL BLOW

"Why are we back here, Mom?" Ellie asked as Anastasia turned the car into the gravel parking lot at Aunt Pat's Restaurant.

Now that Ellie was more awake, she took a long look at the place. The restaurant appeared run down. The red brick showed its age—faded and marked. The wooden roof and railings around the front door revealed chips and scratches. Someone hand painted the sign hanging from the porch roof. It simply said, "Aunt Pat's" in yellowish white. The sidewalk lay cracked and uneven, missing chunks of cement in spots. Weeds grew up all around the building. Ellie knew that didn't matter. Inside, Aunt Pat's was full of love and camaraderie. Friends gathered there. They enjoyed good comfort food. Warm coffee waited. The staff acted like a family.

Anastasia drove to the back of the parking lot and turned the corner behind the building. Garbage lay strewn on the ground. She pointed at the dumpster, sitting partially open at the back corner of the restaurant. "He must have been hiding there, behind the dumpster, watching me as I came out to my car at the end of my shift."

"Who was watching?" Ellie asked.

"Joey," Anastasia said. "It was the day after we went to the movies—the day I slapped him, the same day I met Aaron at the cemetery."

"Why was he watching you from behind the dumpster?"

"I think he was going to try and talk to me, to smooth over what happened the night before, but Aaron showed up. He was driving down the street on his way to meet some friends, and he saw me coming out of work. I think he drove by on purpose, although he'll never admit it." Anastasia smiled. "He saw me walking to my car and beeped his horn. He had an old Ford pickup with a bunch of tools in the back and an archery sticker in the window. It made me smile."

"Doesn't sound much different than what he has now," Ellie said with a laugh.

"That's true," Anastasia grinned. "I waved and he pulled into the parking lot. He said he was happy to see me again and asked what I was doing. I said I was just heading home, nothing exciting. He invited me out for dessert. I asked if I could bring Jessie and he said sure. He offered to pick us up at the house and I accepted. I wrote the address down for him on a piece of my order paper. He offered to swing by within the hour. I was grinning from ear to ear when I turned to get back into my car and head home."

Anastasia put the car in gear and started driving out of the parking lot. Stones shot out from beneath the tires. She turned right and drove three blocks to the apartment building where she had lived. There were three apartments—two downstairs apartments and one big apartment upstairs. The gray-blue siding had not changed since Anastasia lived there as a young woman. Her apartment door sat flush to the road on the west side of the building. She did not have a nice porch or entryway, just a single cement step. Jessie's entrance sat at the back of the house facing the big backyard. She had an awning and small wooden porch with two railings, where she put a single chair and a tiny side table with an ashtray.

"That night I pulled my car up beside my door," Anastasia said, putting the vehicle in park. "Jessie was taking care of the last couple tables. I knew she'd be along soon. I planned on catching her on her way in and telling her about Aaron. She would be up for dessert; anything to meet someone I liked! I went inside, dropped my purse on the love seat, and flicked on the radio. I started looking through my closet, thinking about what I would wear. I pulled out my favorite jeans. They were light blue and had a few fringed holes near the knee. That was the style back then, except you couldn't buy your jeans with pre-made holes," Anastasia said.

Ellie rolled her eyes and smiled. After picking out my clothes, I headed toward the bathroom to take a shower. When I came around the corner into the living room, Joey was standing there. I nearly fainted it scared me so bad. I gasped, but caught my breath quickly and asked him what the hell he was doing.

"I recognized the look in his eyes from some fights my friends had in high school. They called it blacking out. Joey was somewhere else. 'You need to leave my house,' I shouted. 'I'm going to call the police.' I started moving toward the telephone, and he shot at me really fast. I ran in the other direction, toward the bathroom. He ripped the phone cord right out of the wall before turning toward me. He cut me off in the kitchen.

"I had a round wooden table along the kitchen wall. I darted behind it and pushed it forward to put some space between us. He punched the table. I remember screaming, 'What Joey? What did I do to you? Leave me alone!'

"He started laughing and yelled, 'You fucking slut.' He sneered at me. 'You're a stupid whore. You've been leading me on all this time, and then you reject me. Is this a game to you? You think it's funny, toying with people? I saw you with your little boyfriend at the restaurant. Are you getting all dolled up to meet him? You'll probably do the same thing to him. Well, I'm going to save him some pain, you bitch.' With that, Joey threw the table sideways. It crashed against the kitchen cupboards and splintered. A piece of wood flew into the porcelain sink.

"I screamed so loud it hurt my throat. 'Help me! Someone help me!' I knew I was in big trouble.

"Joey tackled me before I could get into the bathroom and threw me down onto the kitchen floor.

He started punching me. After the second or third hit, I don't remember much of anything, except the feeling of something on my neck. I found out later it was his hands. Just before I lost consciousness, I tried to scream. I turned my head sideways. The voice didn't sound like my own. It was horse and croaky. The white linoleum tiles were turning red. I didn't understand why they were red."

Anastasia was looking down at her hands. They were trembling. Ellie grabbed her mother's hands and squeezed them. "Oh my God, Mom," she whispered.

"C'mon, Jessie is going to tell you what happened next," Anastasia said. The girls got out of the car. Jessie had seen them from her window and came down the stairs to the sidewalk to meet them. She nodded at Anastasia and took Ellie by the hand.

"I came home from work that night, maybe five or ten minutes behind Anny," Jessie started. She pulled Ellie toward the door to Anastasia's apartment and the two girls sat down on the cement step.

"Joey locked the door when he went into Anny's place, but I had a key back then. He wouldn't have known that. I slid the door open. It suctioned the air out, making a swooping sound but he didn't hear me."

"I heard Anny scream when I got out of my car. It was an ugly, guttural sound. I knew something was seriously wrong, but I was terrified by what I might find. Then I heard a second voice, a very low voice saying, 'You are getting what's coming to you.' He repeated one word over and over: bitch. Then I would hear a thump, like flesh on flesh. He was beating her."

Jessie continued talking to Ellie as the tears streamed down her cheeks. Anastasia stood beside them, shaking. "I slid the key into the door as quietly as I could. I opened it just a sliver and peeked in. I saw Anny's feet through the kitchen doorway. He was over her, straddling her body with his legs. I saw him heave each time he lifted his arm. Then it stopped. I knew right away he was choking her. I wanted to run, to call the police, but I only had seconds if I was going to save Anny's life."

"There was a little side table by the front door. Anny kept crafts in there. Sometimes she liked to make things while she watched TV at night. I remember she had some kind of cutting tool in there, like a razor blade. I opened the drawer slowly. I didn't want Joey to hear me. I found something better—a long, sharp pair of fabric scissors. They were brand new and shiny. I took the scissors in my hands and tiptoed into the kitchen. Anny's face was changing color. I thought it was too late."

Jessie paused for a moment, crying. She took a few seconds to calm herself, breathing in long, deep breaths. "I crouched for a moment in the doorway, gathering up all of the strength and courage I could muster. I leaped forward, lunging at Joey from behind, and buried the scissors in his back near his shoulder blade. I was aiming for his neck, but the adrenaline had my hands shaking. I missed the mark."

Ellie's eyes were wide with fear.

"He never heard me coming. When the scissors dug into his back, he yelped like a dog. He fell forward, and his hands came off Anny's neck. She sucked in a deep breath, even though she was unconscious. I remember feeling exhilarated. She was alive! Then my victory turned to fear when I realized Joey wasn't down. He had rolled sideways and was grabbing for the scissors. Just as he pulled them out of his skin, he turned to me and rose up from the floor. I knew I was in serious trouble. I was going to run for it. If he chased me, at least Anny would be safe. I started to scream for help. Then Joey's eyes opened really wide, and he put his hand in front of his face. He stopped chasing me and sank back down onto the floor. A loud sound rang out from behind my left ear. I fell and screamed. Something whizzed by me. It was a bullet."

"The shot hit Joey in the chest. They said he died instantly: the bullet entered his heart. I was still trying to run when Aaron grabbed me and lifted me up off the floor. 'It's okay, he's gone,' Aaron whispered in my ear, as the gun fell from his hand onto the floor. 'I need you to find Anastasia's phone and call 911. She looks bad. We need an ambulance.'

"I didn't respond right away, and Aaron shook me. 'I need you to help me,' he yelled. Aaron went straight to Anny's side while I called for help. He sat on the floor Indian style, holding her head in his lap, stroking her hair. I handed him a wet rag and he dabbed the blood from her nose and lips. She was breathing, albeit shallow. We heard the sirens coming down the street. That was when I started to cry. I cried for hours."

Jessie turned around and looked at Anastasia. The two women fell to the sidewalk in a heap, hugging. Ellie jumped in and sat with them, tears streaming down her own face. "I love you, Mom," she repeated over and over. "I love you so much."

HEAD HELD HIGH

Ellie walked down the hallway at Clarksville Central School. Crowds of students moved about in both directions around her. Her long brown hair, which she had curled that morning, tumbled down around her cheeks. It was a softer look than Ellie usually wore. She wore a pair of skinny jeans with a purple tank top and an open, fitted black and white flannel. Her dark brown eyes pierced the questioning glances from her peers. She held her head high and smiled. It was her first time back in the hallways of school since the incident with Casey.

Ellie had realized a number of things since she faced off with her old friend. Perhaps most importantly, she learned that mistakes and pain should never be a source of shame.

"Mistakes are opportunities. They test you, define you," she wrote in her journal the night before. "A person who is good at heart and makes a mistake, does so from a place of not knowing…not knowing how to handle their problems, not knowing where to find the answers, not knowing the implications of their choices. Mistakes bring about knowing."

She drew a little heart in the journal and wrote down her mother's name next to the text. She wrote it the way Jessie always said it—Anny. Below the name she wrote, "I never would have guessed all the times my mom stumbled and fell growing up, precisely because she doesn't hang her head in shame. She squared up her shoulders and moved forward. I admire her for that."

Ellie's reflection continued. "I didn't know so many things, but by making mistakes, I learned. It changed me—permanently. It made me better. I learned its okay to trust people who have had life experiences. Ironically, those are the same people I least trusted with my problems before. In reality, they might actually save me from making more mistakes. They can share all the things they learned along the way."

Now, walking down the hallway of high school, the journal was pressed between her math and English books in her backpack. She wanted to keep it close. About five feet from her locker, Ellie saw Casey approaching. A flash of anxiety flooded her chest, and her heart pounded. It had been about a week since the incident. Casey's black eye had faded to greenish-yellow. She had a sharp red line across her nose where Ellie's fist cut it. Both girls received a week of detention for fighting. Since Ellie took some time off, her week began after Casey's had finished.

Casey received an additional punishment, though. She had to apologize. Ellie thought for sure Casey and her mother would come to the house, to save her from apologizing in school and possibly in front of other students. That could jeopardize the reputation Casey worked so hard to create, but she and her mom never came. The school would inevitably check in with Ellie. Being her first day back, she figured she would hear the apology that day. Now, she looked down the hallway and saw Casey approaching, staring her directly in the eyes, her blonde hair bouncing as she stomped forward. Casey was on a mission.

"Ellie I need to talk to you," she said bluntly. "Can we go in the bathroom?"

Before Ellie could answer, Casey grabbed her arm and swung her around. The girls swerved into the bathroom just a few feet away, which fortunately was empty. Before Casey could get the words out—before they had even turned to look at each other—Ellie reached out her hand and touched Casey's arm.

"I am so sorry that I hit you, Casey. They didn't ask me to apologize, but I want to anyway. I know that you are trying to establish yourself right now and you have big hopes and dreams for high school. I know that we're completely different people. It was okay when we were kids, but we don't care about the same things anymore. I confronted you because I was hurt. You will always be the girl who was my best friend for ten years growing up. Even if we don't hang out anymore, I still care about you. We don't have to be BFFs. What hurt is that you acted like you didn't know me anymore. My hurt turned into anger, and that was not okay. I'm truly sorry."

Casey's eyes glistened as if tears were forming, but she held them back. She didn't speak right away. "I don't want to do this, Ellie," she said in a near-whisper. "I have been so pissed at you this whole week. I planned on saying the words, even if I didn't mean them."

She paused and looked down at the floor. She still looked like the little girl Ellie met in elementary school with the crooked little smile. Whenever Casey got upset she would look down at her feet. Rarely did the words come out. Ellie knew that. She knew what Casey wanted to say.

"It's okay," Ellie spoke in a quiet tone. "Casey, I'll always consider you a dear friend. It's okay we are going separate ways. Just promise me one thing."

Casey let out a deep sigh and looked at Ellie with a half-smile. "What is it?" she asked. This promise would be the forgiveness she needed from Ellie.

"Let's not be mean to each other," said Ellie. "Let's not act like we never met. A hello is enough, no matter who is around. Can we do that?"

Casey's smile grew. "You got it," she said and reached out for a hug.

Ellie obliged.

After that day, Casey delivered on more than her promise. She always said hi, even when her cool friends were around, and sometimes she said, "How are you?" Once in a really great while she'd call Ellie and ask her questions about a homework assignment, which was really a guise to find out about Ellie's life and how things were going. Ellie thought that was just fine.

Ellie found a good group of friends of her own, friends she could relate to. They loved to go on little trips. They went to the aquarium and to the science museum. They were always coming up with creative projects like group sculptures or goofy home videos. They played games a lot and often held study groups before tests. There were boys and girls in the group and one boy in particular, Bruce, that caught Ellie's eye. They flirted innocently and always stayed near to one another. But Ellie's best friend of all was Leann.

Ellie and Leann reconnected the day after Ellie returned from the road trip to Pennsylvania. Ellie decided with her mom to finish out the week at home and return to school the following Monday. The Friday before, she waited until 3:00 and caught a ride into town with her dad. He dropped her off at Leann's house while he ran to the lumberyard. Ellie felt frightened standing outside the house, but her mom assured her Leann wasn't angry. In fact, she'd called five times during their road trip, checking in with Anastasia; hoping Ellie would be ready to talk.

Now the porch looked a mile long and the front door stared ominously back at Ellie. Before she could muster the courage to take the first step, she heard a shriek upstairs. Leann's face peered out of the upstairs window, a huge smile plastered across it and her hand waving furiously. Leann dashed out of her room and down the stairs to the front door, which she flung open carelessly, leaving a little dent in the wall from the door handle. She ran down the porch and leaped off the front steps, wrapping her arms around Ellie in a frantic hug. Ellie laughed out loud.

"Oh my God, Ellie. Your here! You are safe," she shouted.

Ellie had not realized how her trauma had also been Leann's trauma. They went through it together. Perhaps being drugged numbed Ellie's reaction. She had not been completely aware of the severity of it before now, before seeing Leann so relieved.

"I was so scared, Ellie. I've never been so scared in my life. I was sitting in the car when your mom went in that house. I was holding on to the phone, ready to dial 911. I had no idea what would come out of that front door; or not come out." She collapsed back into Ellie's arms and began to cry a little bit—and laugh at the same time.

Ellie took Leann by the arm and led her to the front porch, where she sat her down on the third step. She grabbed her hand. "Leann, I owe you a huge apology. I put you through something really terrible. I have so much to tell you, so much to share with you. We could talk for hours and I couldn't get through it all. For now, though, I want you to know how truly sorry I am. All of this stuff…it changed me, and I promise I will never put you through anything like that again. I hope you will still be my friend."

Leann's tears had dried by then, and she was smiling brightly. "Ellie, I know what kind of a person you are, and I know that you were in a corner. You had no idea how to get yourself out. Your mom and I have talked a lot, and she explained some of it. But all that aside, I knew you before this. You are such a cool girl. From the moment I saw you sitting outside the Guitar Den playing an acoustic waiting for your mom to pick you up, I was like, 'That girl is going to be my friend!' So, I say let's put the past behind us. I am just so happy that you are okay."

"And your parents?" Ellie asked tentatively.

"They talked a lot with your mom too," Leann answered. "Between your mom and I we told them everything. My parents are forgiving people. They want to give you a second chance, Ellie."

Ellie felt a huge pressure lift off of her shoulders and neck. She felt her body relax and the tension in her mind ease away, leaving her eyelids heavy. This was Ellie's moment. She had evolved. The result of her growth meant new friendships and a bright future. High school wasn't going to be that bad after all. Life wasn't going to be that bad. In fact, she dared believe it might even be great. She remembered her mom's story from back in college. She remembered the "little pocket of hope" rising up each time her mom discovered some hidden potential. She felt that way, sitting on Leann's porch. A little pocket of hope rose up inside her. Ellie decided then and there, she wouldn't push it back down. For herself and for her mom, she would let hope rise.